Tailoring PRINCE2

Office of Government Commerce

London: TSO

Published by TSO (The Stationery Office) and available from:

Online
www.tso.co.uk/bookshop

Mail, Telephone, Fax & E-mail
TSO
PO Box 29, Norwich, NR3 1GN
Telephone orders/General enquiries: 0870 600 5522
Fax orders: 0870 600 5533
E-mail: book.orders@tso.co.uk
Textphone 0870 240 3701

TSO Shops
123 Kingsway, London, WC2B 6PQ
020 7242 6393 Fax 020 7242 6394
68-69 Bull Street, Birmingham B4 6AD
0121 236 9696 Fax 0121 236 9699
9-21 Princess Street, Manchester M60 8AS
0161 834 7201 Fax 0161 833 0634
16 Arthur Street, Belfast BT1 4GD
028 9023 8451 Fax 028 9023 5401
18-19 High Street, Cardiff CF10 1PT
029 2039 5548 Fax 029 2038 4347
71 Lothian Road, Edinburgh EH3 9AZ
0870 606 5566 Fax 0870 606 5588

TSO Accredited Agents
(see Yellow Pages)

and through good booksellers

Cover image courtesy of the Royal Scottish National Orchestra: Alexander Lazarev, Principal Conductor.

First published 2002

ISBN 0 11 330897 3

OGC – the Office of Government Commerce – is an office of HM Treasury. Set up in 2000, it incorporates the Central Computer and Telecommunications Agency (CCTA), which no longer operates as a separate agency.

The OGC is now the authority for best practice in commercial activities in UK Government, combining a number of separate functions with related aims.

OGC will build on the popular guidance developed by the former CCTA and others, working with organisations internationally to develop and share business and practitioner guidance within a world-class best prcactice framework.

Printed in the United Kingdom by The Stationery Office.

CONTENTS

FOREWORD

Nowadays, most organisations are experiencing unprecedented levels of change. Change has become a way of life for organisations that need to remain effective and competitive in order to thrive. It is essential to manage the inherent risk associated with change and innovation.

Projects bring together resources, skills, technology and ideas to deliver business benefits or to achieve business objectives. Good project management helps to ensure that these benefits or objectives are achieved within budget, within time and to the required quality.

PRINCE2 is designed to provide a framework covering the wide variety of disciplines and activities required within a project. The focus throughout PRINCE2 is on the business case, which describes the rationale and business justification for the project. The business case drivers all the project management processes, from initial project set-up through to the finish of the project.

PRINCE2 embodies many years of good practice in project management and provides a flexible and adaptable approach to suit all projects.

I commend this *Tailoring PRINCE2* guide to you. May this guide help you to implement PRINCE2 in your organisation and/or to scale PRINCE2 to achieve successful outcomes to your projects!

Bob Assirati
Executive Director
IT Directorate
Office of Government Commerce

ACKNOWLEDGEMENTS

The OGC gratefully acknowledges the contribution Alan Ferguson of AFA Project Management Ltd. has made in compiling this publication.

In addition, it recognises the input of the following individuals, who acted as reviewers:

Brian Swales (The Learning Habit)

Marion Thackwray (Balance Consulting)

John Fisher (Xansa)

Dick Bennett (Abbas Associates)

Bethan Hubbard (Scottish Parliament – user)

Mary Ledgard (Norfolk County Council – user)

Stewart Barrie (user)

1
INTRODUCTION

1.1 'Tailoring' PRINCE2 and the PRINCE2 method

The PRINCE2 project management method is the property of the Office of Government Commerce (OGC), a part of the United Kingdom government. It is encapsulated in the PRINCE2 manual (*Managing Successful Projects with PRINCE2*, TSO (The Stationery Office), 1999, fourth impression (with amendments), ISBN 0 11 330855 8) and supported by a network of accredited training and consultancy organisations throughout the world. The method is used in a variety of different situations worldwide. However, the manual concentrates on describing the method rather than on how it can be used in different situations. Similarly, training tends to focus on the basics of the method rather than on its application. This book is intended to complement the PRINCE2 manual by giving guidance on how the method can be applied.

1.2 Familiarity with PRINCE2

It is assumed that the reader already has a working knowledge of PRINCE2; its concepts are therefore not repeated here. This book is aimed at a reader who has been trained to practitioner level and is in current practice. Practitioners who have not used the method for some time may find it useful to have a PRINCE2 manual available.

For those who have not undertaken training to practitioner level it is recommended that they attend an approved training course or seek the support of an approved PRINCE2 consultant.

1.3 Who should read this book?

This book is intended for those who are:

- moving into active project management, having taken PRINCE2 exams
- using PRINCE2 on a single project
- using PRINCE2 on a series of projects
- keen to import elements of PRINCE2 to improve control and the management of risk in a non-PRINCE2 environment
- introducing PRINCE2 as a site standard.

The book will refer to each of these as a PRINCE2 champion. There is no suggestion that this is a formally recognised appointment, neither is it linked to a particular project role. A champion may be an employee or an external consultant. For simplicity, projects will usually be viewed from the Project Manager's point of view.

1.4 What this book aims to do

'Tailoring PRINCE2' can be taken to mean using PRINCE2 appropriately. This book aims to assist the PRINCE2 champion to implement the method in an organisation and/or scale PRINCE2 in a project. Scaling the method involves a judgement on how extensively to use an element of PRINCE2 within a single project. Implementing the method involves consideration of the circumstances within one project in the light of the culture of a particular line organisation and the history of PRINCE2 in that organisation. Consequently, tailoring PRINCE2 involves implementing the method, to a greater or lesser extent, and scaling it.

It is relatively straightforward to scale up PRINCE2. The PRINCE2 manual describes each of the elements in detail. Also, approved consultants or internal PRINCE2 experts can be recruited to assist on large projects. Therefore, this book will concentrate on scaling down PRINCE2 – using PRINCE2 elements with a lightness of touch, when appropriate.

1.5 Terminology

This book uses initial capitals for PRINCE2-specific terminology. For example, 'Role' refers to one of the roles within a PRINCE2 Project Management team; 'Organisation' refers to a PRINCE2 component while 'organisation', 'line organisation' or 'background organisation' refer to a business or service that is participating in one or more projects. An organisation may be of any size and may be a department or division within a larger body. PRINCE2 processes, components and techniques together are referred to as elements.

1.6 Structure of *Tailoring PRINCE2*

1.6.1 Sequence of chapters

This book first considers various aspects of implementing PRINCE2, including:

- the steps an organisation should take when implementing PRINCE2
- alignment of PRINCE2 with corporate working practices and power bases
- PRINCE2 by stealth
- standards, templates and tools

- the Project Support Office
- the maturing PRINCE2 organisation.

Then the book covers scaling PRINCE2:

- types of project
- various approaches to scaling.

Finally, implementing and scaling each PRINCE2 process, component and technique is covered in detail.

Those charged with introducing PRINCE2 may care to read the early chapters on implementing it. Readers charged with supporting PRINCE2 on sites that have already adopted the method will find the chapters on scaling PRINCE2 particularly useful. The practitioner seeking focused support on one element of PRINCE2 should consult the later chapters.

1.6.2 Structure of each section

The body of this book has been structured to provide the reader with a light and powerful reference guide. Across double-page spreads, the book provides self-contained guidance to each particular aspect of implementing or scaling PRINCE2. Each section has a broadly similar layout that is likely to include the following.

1.6.2.1 Cross-references to the PRINCE2 method

The first section contains cross-references to the PRINCE2 method. These are not references to particular pages or chapters in the manual. In different impressions of the PRINCE2 manual, amendments have led to changes of page numbering and the order of chapters. This book provides a cross-reference that can be used with a variety of editions of the PRINCE2 manual. It assumes that readers are familiar with the practice of referring to PRINCE2 processes and components by their initials, for example 'DP1' signifies 'Directing a Project – Authorising Initiation'. This approach is used throughout this book.

The method is more than just the words in a manual. By cross-referring to the PRINCE2 method, this book emphasizes the importance of the ideas underpinning the method.

1.6.2.2 Examples

Within most sections of the book a 'real life' example of the activity under discussion is usually provided. These examples may be best practice or may be an example of how inappropriate handling of a situation led to difficulties.

1.6.2.3 Scaling

In each section, advice is included that will help the practitioner to decide the most appropriate way of scaling PRINCE2 to the project in hand.

1.6.2.4 Implementing

As well as, or instead of, giving narrow scaling advice, the book includes guidance on implementation of PRINCE2 according to the local culture and circumstances.

1.7 Best practice

As the guardians of the PRINCE2 method, OGC commissioned *Tailoring PRINCE2* so that it would reflect examples of current, proven best practice rather than the views of any one individual or group. Therefore, the author was asked to carry out the widest possible consultation exercise.

The author called on the services of a group of reviewers who had worked together on sister publications. He also made use of the experience of the accredited training community, which conducts PRINCE2 training throughout the world. Further, the Prince User Group was contacted and its members polled for their experiences. These covered private and public sector projects from around the world, involving IT, engineering, organisational development and change management specialists. Finally, a feedback session was conducted at a Prince User Group meeting to ensure that the messages in the book represented best practice.

Following publication of the first edition of this book, the process of consultation and debate will continue and further editions will be published, if appropriate.

The PRINCE2 manual is designed to be rigorously consistent across its different parts. This book has gathered experience from a wide range of sites, in the public and private sectors and internationally. While each of these examples is consistent with PRINCE2, they represent widely different circumstances. Therefore, the advice given in one section may conflict with the advice in another because it applies to different circumstances. Consequently, it would be wrong to quote this book as an authority for acting in one way or another regardless of the circumstances.

1.8 Risks and effort associated with implementation of structured methods

The purist would argue that implementing structured project management involves no effort and no risk. However, in reality, an organisation must make a concerted effort when changing its project management culture, and there are significant risks associated with changing a culture. One needs to understand these risks and costs so that they can be controlled. As with risk management within a project, if the risks are managed they will not come to fruition. Addressing these risks frankly enables the PRINCE2 champion to manage them.

The PRINCE2 method makes clear that the Project Management team must make choices about how comprehensively to use each element of PRINCE2. The manual implies that these choices are solely based on the characteristics of the project. Taking a broader view, there are additional factors to be borne in mind.

1.8.1 The effect of costs of implementation

The experience level and familiarity of the team with project management methods is significant. The term 'team' means not just a Project Management team, but also the wider group of individuals who are impacted by the project. If an individual is familiar and confident with a particular technique then he or she will use it more often.

The Business Case for using an element of PRINCE2 will be improved if the cost of using the management product, technique or process is lower. Inexperienced staff will take longer to do the same piece of work therefore the cost will be higher. Consequently, there will be circumstances where it would be appropriate for an experienced practitioner, for example, to fully document a Project Issue. It might not be appropriate for an inexperienced practitioner to do so if the cost would outweigh the benefits. This is the justification for using PRINCE2 less intensively in an environment where there is limited experience.

1.8.2 Balancing risk

Another factor is the forbearance of an inexperienced team. A group that is familiar with PRINCE2 will be happy to make full use of, say, a process because they appreciate how it will contribute to the successful completion of the project. An inexperienced group may be more cautious. (Further coverage of how different types of people may respond is found in *People Issues and PRINCE2* (TSO (The Stationery Office), 2002, ISBN 0 11 330896 5).)

During Start Up. The Project Manager and Executive should design the Project Management team. An experienced Project Manager might do this by running through the key criteria for SU2 as a series of questions to be put to his or her new Executive. An experienced Executive would be happy to run through the full set of questions because they appreciated the advantages of a soundly designed Project Management team. An inexperienced Executive might be less willing to spend so much time on designing the team. So, as an experienced Project Manager poses the questions, he or she senses irritation from across the desk. What should the Project Manager do? If the Manager presses on with the full set of questions he or she might alienate their new Executive. However, if he or she fails to pose some of the questions there could be negative consequences downstream.

This is an example of a project risk being managed. The risk stems from the inexperience of the Executive, a risk that is very real. There are a number of possible outcomes. The Project Manager needs to evaluate the potential adverse impact of each of these outcomes in terms of their likely consequences. The Project Manager must then decide how to manage these risks. One of the common outcomes is that the Project Manager holds back on the last few questions. Consequently, a poorly designed Project Management team is put in place.

Is this 'full PRINCE2'? This book argues that it is. The culture of the organisation over many years has led to the Executive not gaining experience of PRINCE2 projects. Consequently, the risk of the Executive becoming irritated by questions from the Project Manager is a real one. In this case, the Executive's irritation outweighs the risk of failing to put in place a thoroughly designed Project Management team. Therefore, in terms of risk management, the Project Manager is absolutely right to back off.

When using PRINCE2 in an immature environment the experienced champion is constantly facing this sort of dilemma. He or she realise it would be appropriate to put in place a more rigorous implementation of PRINCE2, however that might create unacceptable risks, given the background culture. Therefore, the champion must play down some elements of PRINCE2.

2

IMPLEMENTING PRINCE2

On a training course everything seems so logical and straightforward. But the following week, back at work, it all seems much more difficult. The same is true of PRINCE2. During PRINCE2 courses, trainers make it all seem so easy, yet in the office it can seem impossibly difficult to start using the PRINCE2 method. However, the seed of that difficulty is often sown long before staff are sent on a training course. Implementing PRINCE2 consists of much more than just staff training.

This chapter considers what an organisation should do in order to implement PRINCE2. The aim is to implement PRINCE2 successfully without disrupting the normal flow of work.

The difference between a project and day-to-day work will be briefly considered. Routine work can be viewed as a series of processes. These should not be confused with PRINCE2 processes, which were created precisely to make projects more predictable, more routine.

A model is described showing how people with various levels of experience have to be managed in different ways. So, an understanding of the type of support environment that has to be put in place if newly trained staff are to use PRINCE2 quickly and effectively should be the final outcome of this chapter.

2.1 Projects and processes

Figure 2.1 illustrates how projects offer a fundamentally different management environment from day-to-day processes.

Line organisations have evolved from a process background. Their cultures encourage and reward the creation of successful processes. Staff will have developed in an environment where the creation and maintenance of processes results in advancement.

When staff move to a project environment they must adopt a different set of priorities. This transition may be reasonably straightforward for junior and inexperienced staff who might move to full-time project roles. The situation is much more difficult for senior staff. They are likely to have more experience of a process culture and will regard it as a successful way of doing business. Furthermore, they are likely to split their time between a process culture and a project culture. To migrate fully to a project culture a variety of aids need to be put in place to assist staff to operate in that culture, which are described below.

Figure 2.1 Project and process management

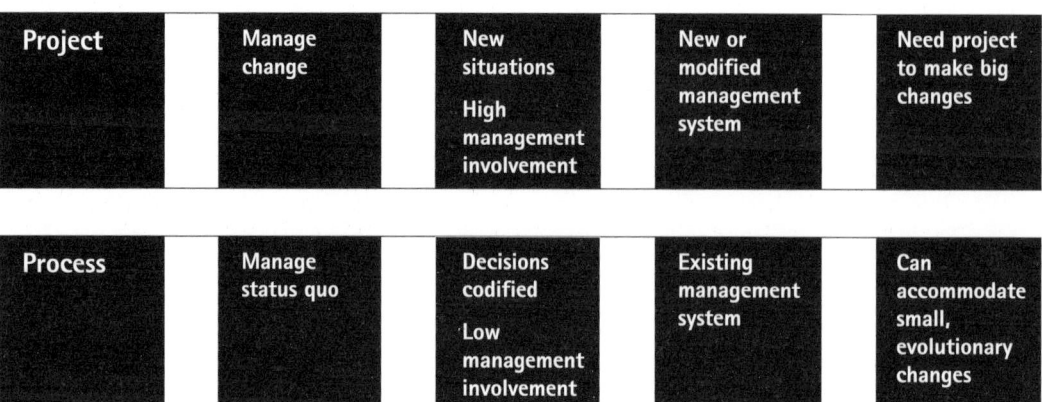

Project		Manage change		New situations High management involvement		New or modified management system		Need project to make big changes
Process		Manage status quo		Decisions codified Low management involvement		Existing management system		Can accommodate small, evolutionary changes

2.2 Support styles

Figure 2.2 shows how the levels of competence and commitment of staff vary as they acquire a new skill, such as the application of PRINCE2.

As they move along this path they will need different levels of support and direction. Support involves listening, encouraging and facilitating, while direction is about telling others how, where and when to do something and then closely supervising their performance. Furthermore, the level of support and direction that is given to them will subconsciously tell them how the organisation perceives their development.

Figure 2.2 Support styles

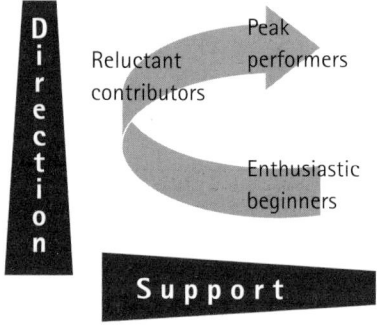

How people react to different types of management support and direction is discussed in *People Issues and PRINCE2* (TSO (The Stationery Office), 2002, ISBN 0 11 330896 5).

2.2.1 Enthusiastic beginners

The enthusiastic beginner is likely to have a high level of commitment but a low level of competence. They will require a high degree of direction but a much lower level of support or encouragement. Staff in this situation often react favourably to training courses, which are a highly directive environment. They will accept the introduction of a manual and welcome the publication of mandatory procedures. Staff with a low level of knowledge expect to be treated in a similar manner and therefore accept and even welcome attending a training course together.

Senior staff may not wish to be regarded as enthusiastic beginners as they may perceive this as undermining their status. Consequently, they may be too busy to attend training courses. Once on a training course, they might attempt to reinforce their status by questioning manuals and local procedures. Senior staff who might react in this manner may need to be trained in a different environment. Perhaps amongst their peers, but separated from their subordinates, they will explore new ideas. It may be politic to call such an event a seminar or workshop rather than a training course.

2.2.2 Disillusioned learners

As staff begin to apply and develop a newly acquired skill they need increasing levels of support, balanced by less prescriptive direction. This is the typical situation staff find themselves in when they return from a training course.

An organisation attempting to implement PRINCE2 should ensure that staff returning from a training course are given an increased level of support. This could involve coaching and mentoring. Newly trained staff will support one another, but their skill levels will be low and therefore this could be inefficient. Mentors should be proficient in the application of PRINCE2. As a temporary expedient, support may have to be provided by external consultants or experts based in a Project Support Office.

This is also the correct time to introduce tools such as templates or software packages, but only if proficient people are available who understand how they should operate. Proficient staff can be concentrated in a Project Support Office.

2.2.3 Reluctant contributors

Reluctant contributors will have made some progress in developing their newly acquired skills but may be reaching a plateau. As such, they require a high level of support and encouragement but a much lower level of direction.

Characteristically, the reluctant contributor's opinion of PRINCE2 fluctuates. When positive, they may claim that it is what they have always done and is just common sense. When encountering difficulties while applying the method, they might claim that the method itself is flawed.

Reluctant contributors are likely to be well respected and therefore their opinions cannot be dismissed. However, their fluctuating attitude to PRINCE2 may actually reveal their underlying lack of confidence in their ability to master the method.

The key to managing the reluctant contributor is to employ a variety of approaches. They should be brought within the PRINCE2 community; their opinion as experienced project practitioners should be sought. They can be asked to carry out project audits, or to comment on how individual elements of PRINCE2 mesh with local circumstances or procedures. When they are less positive, these techniques can be used to constrain their reluctance. If they have carried out audits they will find it difficult to resist being audited themselves. If they have contributed to the implementation of PRINCE2 they will find it more difficult to distance themselves from the method. Thus, they can be contained without being alienated.

2.2.4 Peak performers

Peak performers need very low levels of either support or direction. Indeed, they may find it insulting to be given higher levels of support or direction. It is inappropriate and ineffective to manage peak performers by requiring them to comply with individual elements of PRINCE2. The PRINCE2 method has a comprehensive set of management products that are produced at the end of the project. These can be used to confirm that the project has been delivered in accordance with the Project Initiation Document and Business Case. Peak performers, therefore, should be audited and rewarded solely by checking Lessons Learned Reports, End Project Reports, Follow-on Action Recommendations and Post-Project Reviews.

2.3 An implementation strategy

These caricatures may be rather simplistic, but they serve to illustrate that those wishing to implement PRINCE2 should not merely commission a series of training courses. In addition, the champion needs to consider support mechanisms such as mentors, procedures, templates and standards; audit, plus empowerment mechanisms involving local tailoring; and performance-based reward.

2.3.1 Training

Training is an extremely important way of acquiring a working knowledge of the PRINCE2 method. PRINCE2 champions need to have a sound working knowledge of the method. This can be obtained by attending an accredited practitioner course provided by one of the many

Accredited Training Organisations (ATOs). A list of these can be found on the APMG website at www.prince2.org.uk.

Successful users of PRINCE2 invariably put in place a mixture of training courses, ranging from overviews to practitioner training. This training may be tailored in-house or an open course, but some form of training at least is essential. Nevertheless, as this chapter illustrates, training is just the first step in implementing PRINCE2.

2.3.2 Support

Training needs to be followed up with sufficient support to rapidly raise the productivity of staff adopting the new PRINCE2 procedures. This is likely to cover a range of topics including:

- access to coaches or mentors who are themselves experienced in the use of PRINCE2
- clear, mature procedures for using PRINCE2 in the local environment
- templates
- tools.

Ideally, staff should not have access to these support procedures prior to their training but should have full access immediately after training. It is rarely possible to sequence events so precisely, nevertheless the PRINCE2 implementation team should aim for support to be available immediately after staff training.

2.3.3 Audit

While training and support can be rolled out through existing administration functions, a PRINCE2 implementation team can expect compliance issues to arise soon after the initial adoption of PRINCE2. Some managers may be reluctant to adopt PRINCE2, for reasons that may or may not be valid; while others may use PRINCE2 inappropriately. Time will have to be spent working with reluctant contributors in an attempt to change their attitudes. In addition, audits should be scheduled and resourced to measure, objectively, the success of the adoption of PRINCE2. It should be anticipated that management effort will have to be expended on handling both sets of issues.

2.3.4 Reward

Consideration may also have to be given to the potential benefits from modifying pay and reward procedures. Rewarding those using PRINCE2, in a manner that leads to project success and is in accordance with the local implementation, is a powerful incentive.

2.3.5 The PRINCE2 implementation project

The PRINCE2 champion should put in place a balance of:

- **training**
- **procedures and templates**
- **audit mechanisms**
- **performance-based reward.**

Furthermore, champions should carry out an analysis of the people who will be using PRINCE2 in order to identify the appropriate way in which each of them should be managed. Such a widely based initiative should be managed in conjunction with line managers and the human resources department, and can even be treated as a pilot PRINCE2 project.

The Business Case for such a project can easily be made by claiming for the PRINCE2 implementation a proportion of the benefits of projects being managed under PRINCE2. The proportion claimed should be based on factors such as the earlier availability of benefits because of reduced delays. Ideally, the implementing organisation should first benchmark their project productivity against others. This type of exercise has been difficult to carry out, historically, not least because an organisation that is thinking of introducing PRINCE2 may not have consistent metrics on project performance. If rigorous benchmarking is impractical a less rigorous argument may be used. Broadly speaking, projects still tend to overrun initial estimates by the order of 100% when changes in time, scope, resource, quality and risk are taken into account. If adoption of PRINCE2 can achieve, say, a nominal 5% improvement in project performance, the benefits of adoption are likely to far outweigh the costs.

Champions may also wish to consider commissioning an external audit by accredited PRINCE2 management consultants to confirm that their implementation strategy is sound. A list of these is available at www.prince2.org.uk.

3
FITTING IN

PRINCE2 is project-centric: the method focuses on a project, and routine operations are seen as an external influence. However, some users of PRINCE2 may see routine work as the dominant factor and their project may be perceived as a temporary aberration.

This chapter considers PRINCE2 from the perspective of an existing line organisation. It considers how PRINCE2 must complement that existing culture if it is to become established. It describes how PRINCE2 interfaces with the background culture in areas such as corporate quality systems, Configuration Management standards, the organisational hierarchy, budgeting and project approval processes, and management by objectives. A further section expands on the part of the method that covers PRINCE2 in a commercial environment.

This chapter also looks at the dangers posed by implementing PRINCE2 within a business. There are risks associated with introducing any new method, but the risks of implementing PRINCE2 can be outweighed by the advantages of improved project performance.

Finally, the situation where it is impractical to launch PRINCE2 as an overt initiative is considered. For many reasons, it may be best to simply make use of PRINCE2 as generic best practice without specifically referring to the method.

3.1 PRINCE2 and existing organisational features

3.1.1 Corporate quality systems

3.1.1.1 Cross-reference to the PRINCE2 method

- Quality component and, in particular, the concepts of Quality Systems, the Quality Path, ISO 9001 and Quality Assurance

3.1.1.2 Example

Some IT staff in a government agency adopted PRINCE2. However, there was resistance from another more powerful group within the IT department. As a result of the subsequent debates about the value and relevance of PRINCE2, the initiative stalled.

A separate, non-IT, Quality Assurance department reported directly to the chief executive. The head of the Quality Assurance department became aware of the discussions about PRINCE2 so he commissioned a review of a number of IT projects, which led to a recommendation that structured methods should be adopted. As a consequence, the introduction of PRINCE2 received backing from the wider business community. The group within IT that had been slowing the introduction of PRINCE2 then decided to drop their opposition.

By enlisting the support of a corporate Quality Assurance department, PRINCE2 champions succeeded in overcoming local resistance to the method.

3.1.1.3 Implementing

The quality system/culture of Customer and Supplier line organisations are represented on the Quality Path diagram as lying outside the project boundary. Nevertheless, the influence of a Quality Assurance department may be significant when implementing PRINCE2.

What PRINCE2 would consider to be a Quality Assurance function may take many forms. Internal Audit sections frequently have a broad remit that extends their role beyond financial compliance into Quality Assurance. Standards departments may similarly have a wide-ranging and proactive role.

The PRINCE2 champion should take time to understand if the documented corporate quality system is the same as the actual, informal systems that operate day to day. Care should be taken to map the Quality component onto the terminology and processes that already exist. There is a detailed cross-reference between PRINCE2 and ISO 9001 in earlier versions of the PRINCE2 manual. It is a useful example of how such mapping can be carried out.

PRINCE2 should not be presented as a competitor to the Quality Assurance regime as that could alienate a Quality Assurance department. Quality Assurance staff can contribute to the Project Assurance role, monitoring how quality checks are specified and carried out and encouraging compliance with PRINCE2.

Many organisations have powerful and well-established Quality Assurance departments, often reporting directly to the most senior level. These bodies can be powerful allies when attempting to implement PRINCE2.

3.1.2 Configuration Management standards

3.1.2.1 Cross-reference to the PRINCE2 method

- Configuration Management component

3.1.2.2 Example

In a project with a commercial Customer/Supplier environment, the Customer was relatively new to structured project management, while the Supplier had considerable experience in the field. The Supplier Team Manager was surprised when presented with the Project Brief, apparently under rigorous Configuration Management. There was a page of document revision details and version numbering embedded in fields in the footer. When the Customer amended the Project Brief, none of these details were updated and the file version number was not changed. The Supplier queried this and the Customer Project Manager admitted that the template was one they had been given. She agreed she had little appreciation of how it should be used.

3.1.2.3 Implementing

Many sites have existing standards for Configuration Management. Management of document-based Configuration Items ranges from the use of version numbers in footers, through document property sheets and audit trails on the front pages of documents, to document management systems. Specialist product Configuration Management standards are usually embedded within various areas of the parent organisation and are beyond the scope of this book. That said, specialist products can range from IT software to the skills and knowledge of individuals. In general, standards for the control of specialist products also range from the non-existent to the sophisticated. This wide range means that it is impracticable to be specific about Configuration Management standards.

It is often illuminating for the PRINCE2 champion to look at the existing standards and how rigorously they are complied with. **Frequently, sites have complex Configuration Management standards that are simply not enforced. There may be an opportunity to simplify standards, and put a little additional effort into enforcing them, in order to ensure that documents or other products are kept properly under configuration control.** PRINCE2 is then likely to be perceived as both supporting and improving local standards.

3.1.3 Organisation hierarchies

3.1.3.1 Cross-reference to the PRINCE2 method

● Organisation component

3.1.3.2 Example

A company specialised in undertaking large Work Packages as a subcontractor on larger projects. They provided a manager to work full-time on these assignments who effectively acted as a PRINCE2 Team Manager. The company also put in place a more senior relationship manager with a technical background.

The company wished to appoint the relationship manager to the Project Board. However, some Senior Suppliers resisted this, leaving the relationship manager with no defined role. Consequently, it was difficult to differentiate the project roles of the relationship and Team managers. Sometimes the relationship manager would usurp the authority of the Team Manager by intervening directly with the Project Manager or Board.

3.1.3.3 Implementing

PRINCE2 makes no allowance for middle managers in the chain of command between the Project Manager and members of the Project Board. Nor does it cater for the superiors of Team Managers from a commercial subcontractor.

There can be strong pressure to give middle managers a project role. This can be for the best or worst of reasons. The middle managers may be more capable and in tune with the wider picture; alternatively, they may simply wish to maintain their status, and to filter and control communication between the Project Manager and the Project Board.

The narrow interests of the project are best served by direct communication between the Project Manager and the Project Board on the one hand, and the Project Manager and Team Managers on the other.

Giving middle managers a Project Assurance role that clears the way for direct communication between the Project Manager and the Project Board or Team Managers can accommodate the need for them to remain involved.

If more comprehensive alterations to the Project Management structure are necessary, the reasons for these compromises should be clearly documented in the Project Initiation Document.

3.1.4 Budgeting and project approval processes

3.1.4.1 Cross-reference to the PRINCE2 method

- Business Case component

3.1.4.2 Example

Governments mostly operate an annual budgeting cycle. The Business Case for small projects may be funded from generic budget headings. For larger projects, specific budget allocation, quite properly, needs to be made. If provisional bids have not been made in advance such allocations can only be put into a subsequent financial year. Consequently, it can take up to 12 months for a Business Case to be funded. This means a Controlled Start for relatively modest projects can take over a year.

3.1.4.3 Implementing

While the PRINCE2 method implies that processes may be short – a matter of hours or days – this is not stated explicitly. For wider reasons, there can be lags of many months between some processes, particularly at the beginning of projects.

Many organisations, whether in the public or commercial sectors, will have funding rules set by finance departments. Projects must operate within these funding rules, which means there can be a hiatus before the approval of a Business Case. This can occur during either Start Up or Initiation, depending on how the term 'Outline Business Case' is interpreted.

A procedure for the approval of Business Cases is one example of a mechanism for prioritising projects. Other prioritisation procedures may also exist. If a programme management environment exists, this prioritisation will take place in a setting that is closely related to the project environment. Where no programme environment exists, project advocates will need to comply with both Business Case and project approval processes as projects move from conception through to a Controlled Start.

Budgeting and project approval processes may radically alter the timescale of projects, but both are inevitable and fully justified when viewed in the wider context of a business or public service.

The PRINCE2 champion should allow for these processes when planning the start of a project. More work may have to be done on the Business Case during Start Up, and the duration of Start Up or Initiation may be increased.

3.1.5 Management by Exception

3.1.5.1 Cross-reference to the PRINCE2 method

- Concept of Management by Exception – which underlies various controls, particularly Tolerance

3.1.5.2 Example

A long-serving departmental director was in the habit of checking the work of subordinates at a very low level of detail. He continued with this approach when acting as Executive on Project Boards. He would insist that the full details of stages were submitted to him in advance of Project Boards. At the Board, he would then cross-question all present on the lowest levels of detail within the plan, even if the project was well within Tolerance.

Over time, Project Managers did not even attempt to proactively manage stages. They simply reacted to the inevitable questions that would be put by the Executive. Decision-making within projects became paralysed, as all matters were referred to that individual. Nevertheless, he claimed to be using PRINCE2.

3.1.5.3 Implementing

Management by Exception lies at the core of PRINCE2. From it stems the concepts of Stages, Tolerance and Highlights. In turn, these ideas allow a relatively senior Project Board to direct a much more junior Project Manager. Consequently, a Project Manager can have access to the decision-makers who provide him or her with resources. In short, many of the PRINCE2 inter-relationships stem from Management by Exception.

Nevertheless, many successful organisations and senior managers do not operate a regime of Management by Exception. They are reluctant to delegate and instead manage their subordinates by examining their work in detail. This type of manager will not even agree that there is a level of detail below which they will not intervene. At some point, these very high levels of senior management intervention mean that a substantial portion of PRINCE2 is not being applied. The PRINCE2 champions should encourage the adoption of Management by Exception wherever possible. Pragmatically, they may have to accept that Management by Exception may not be used if senior managers are unwilling to change their style.

In such circumstances, PRINCE2 stages shrink in size. It may be possible to interpret a weekly detailed review meeting as a form of verbal Highlight Report. Such a meeting will actually be a Stage Boundary, if the Project Board approves a new or significantly altered Stage Plan at the meeting.

3.1.6 The commercial environment

3.1.6.1 Cross-references to the PRINCE2 method

- Quality Path within the Quality component
- Organisation component
- Risk component

3.1.6.2 Example

This example was illustrated in a documentary, produced by the BBC in the *Horizon* series, concerning the production of the Boeing 777 aircraft.

Traditionally, aircraft designers have accepted orders for a new aircraft type and then developed the aircraft with very limited involvement from their customers. During the development of the Boeing 777 the company took a deliberate decision to involve the User community in the aircraft's development.

The critical factor was aircraft weight and the Supplier had guaranteed a particular aircraft weight. A heavy part was overweight. This would consume the last of the weight contingency and the project was about to go into Exception. In one scene, the Project Manager was chairing a meeting to examine this issue. The discomfort on the faces of the Boeing employees, who were being forced to discuss weight growth in front of the customers, was most vivid.

Once the subject had been aired an engineer from an airline joined in the discussion. He suggested that because of the way the Users would operate this product, a particular feature on the component could be omitted. If that feature were omitted the part could be made lighter. A solution had been found because the User community had been involved in assessing the Issue.

When the prototype aircraft was rolled out, the legend inscribed under the cockpit was 'Working Together'. PRINCE2 projects could choose no better theme.

3.1.6.3 Implementing

Traditional commercial practice acts as a barrier between the Customer and Supplier. There is then a tendency for information not to be shared between the two camps.

An example of a lack of openness is the idea of a Customer Risk Log and a Supplier Risk Log. Great care must be taken in the use of Supplier Risk Logs. When a risk is only recorded within the Supplier community, the management of the risk is not being handled by the project but only by the Supplier team, even if the User community may be able to assist with the management of the risk.

Furthermore, the Supplier will have to have made allowance for the cost of managing the risk and the possible cost of the risk occurring, within the Supplier Business Case. Suppliers will, at a minimum, cover the potential costs associated with the risk occurring. Therefore, leaving risks within the Supplier community will be an additional cost on the Customer. This additional cost will dilute the Customer's – the Project's – Business Case. Customers may choose to do this if they wish to transfer risks, but they should be party to these decisions.

Some argue that this confrontational approach is a commercial necessity. Yet, there are numerous examples of projects that have failed and have led to significant commercial losses because of such secrecy.

PRINCE2 is based on an open dialogue and partnership between the Customer and Supplier. This principle is enacted within the Quality Path. Specifically, it is in the formulation of a joint Project Quality Plan and a chain of Product Descriptions that do not differentiate between Customer and Supplier staff. When this openness is successfully established, Product Descriptions and products pass freely between the Customer and Supplier communities on a regular and frequent basis. Indeed, the aim is to form cross-functional teams with a broad skill base that do not differentiate between Customer and Supplier loyalties. These aspirations may sound naïve but experience shows they can be implemented.

The PRINCE2 champion is unlikely to be in a position to change the commercial culture of a Supplier. However, the champion may care to consider that commercial confidentiality is likely to work against the best interests of a project. If champions are from the Customer community, they could seek greater disclosure during contract negotiations. If they are Suppliers, they could plan for more frequent releases to the Customer.

In summary, confidential management products may work against the interests of the Customer, the Supplier or both parties. The two parties should therefore agree how their use will be constrained.

3.2 Managing the risks associated with a limited implementation of PRINCE2

3.2.1 Cross-reference to the PRINCE2 method

- An element of the Risk component, but applicable throughout the method

3.2.2 Example

A PRINCE2 consultant was assisting a client to define the project organisation. The Executive wished to appoint a specialist manager as deputy Project Manager. Although this individual's post and seniority qualified him to be a Project Manager, he did not support the project and had a reputation for stifling innovation.

The consultant advised the Executive to appoint the specialist to an Assurance role instead, however the Executive was adamant. The consultant was now in a quandary: he could foresee problems for the project, but recognised that the Executive would not alter his view.

He wrote a confidential note to the Executive expressing his concerns and then worked with the deputy Project Manager to try to make the project a success. After a difficult six months, the specialist manager was moved to a Project Assurance role.

3.2.3 Implementing

Failing to implement elements of PRINCE2 with sufficient rigour leads to less effective projects. Yet, sometimes a champion may have to accept such a situation.

If a PRINCE2 champion recognises that an element of the method is necessary for the successful execution of a project, failure to implement that element of PRINCE2 could lead to a risk that the project would be less successful. For clarity we will call this an omission risk.

On the other hand, if adoption of an element of PRINCE2 would cause an adverse reaction in the line culture, the possibility of the adverse reaction is also a risk – an adverse reaction risk. The adverse reaction may not be logical: PRINCE2 may simply have a poor reputation, or the adverse reaction could be founded in internal politics. For example, if one group were supporting PRINCE2, another group might therefore wish to oppose its introduction. An organisation might also be opposed to the concept of structured project management in general. Alternatively, there might be reasons why an organisation does not wish to recognise that projects are different.

Whatever the circumstances, there are two risks to be balanced: an omission risk of not implementing an element of PRINCE2, and the risk of an adverse reaction if the element is implemented.

The PRINCE2 champion should put in place appropriate management of the risks. The first step is to carry out risk analysis on the two risks. The champion should compare the impact of the two risks and may also have to look at a possible countermeasure before deciding whether to implement the element of PRINCE2 or not. One risk will then be prevented; the other risk will have to be managed, so the countermeasure will have to be planned, resourced, monitored and controlled. One should then document this decision, albeit in a Risk Log with a limited circulation. Alternatively, it might be prudent only to document the action in the PRINCE2 champion's personal Daily Log.

Should the risk occur, the consequences can be examined in the Lessons Learned Report or the End Project Report, and the Post-Project Review if the risk has affected the Business Case. Positive conclusions should be drawn that can be fed back into subsequent projects.

In an organisation that is new to PRINCE2, this situation is very common. The PRINCE2 champion often has to back down from implementing some elements of PRINCE2 because of forecast adverse reactions. This should not be regarded as a defeat or victory rather as part of the natural learning process inherent when an organisation absorbs structured project management.

3.3 PRINCE2 by stealth

3.3.1 Cross-reference to the PRINCE2 method

- Applicable throughout the method

3.3.2 Example

A consultant, who was a PRINCE2 practitioner, was undertaking a general consultancy assignment for a client, to create an Information Systems (IS) strategy. The client had not adopted PRINCE2, therefore it was not used formally to manage the project. However, the consultant did use significant elements of PRINCE2 when appropriate.

After about six months the client decided to adopt PRINCE2 and, coincidentally, the consultant's main contact was nominated to provide User Assurance on the project to implement PRINCE2. Naturally, he went on a PRINCE2 training course and was surprised when he found that he was familiar with some of the PRINCE2 concepts. On his return from the training course he challenged the consultant, who admitted that he had been using PRINCE2 by stealth. The consultant and client then reviewed some of the events during the strategy project and saw how elements of PRINCE2 had been applied. The client was pleased to see that PRINCE2 was usable in a realistic environment and became a vociferous advocate of the adoption of PRINCE2.

3.3.3 Implementing

PRINCE2 is a complementary framework of elements. These elements are based on common sense and the collective experience of the PRINCE2 community.

Much of the strength of PRINCE2 comes from the interlocking synergy of the elements: the individual elements support and reinforce one another. In turn, this has led to the evolution of a precise vocabulary so that the same terms have consistent meanings within different elements. Paradoxically, the existence of this standard vocabulary can be a hurdle to the adoption of PRINCE2. People can sometimes view a new vocabulary as an imposition and an external threat. There may also be preconceived and negative notions about PRINCE2.

If there is resistance to the adoption of PRINCE2, the PRINCE2 champion can instead adopt individual elements as examples of generic best practice without ever making specific reference to the method – PRINCE2 by stealth. So, for example, if asked to draft the specific responsibilities for an individual managing a project, a PRINCE2 champion could put forward some or all of the specific responsibilities of a PRINCE2 Project Management team role. Similarly, Product Description outlines are very useful as templates for management products, even if the term 'management products' is not recognised within the culture.

Care needs to be taken over the casual introduction of PRINCE2 vocabulary. Because this specific vocabulary is so carefully defined some if it will not be in common use. For example, the term Project Manager is widely used, but Project Board is not yet so well known. The champion may have to use a more familiar term such as 'steering committee', while trying to avoid the indecisiveness of large committees. If vocabulary is altered, the amended vocabulary should be used consistently. This will generate additional effort for the champion. The existence of amended vocabulary will also create a training task and will make it harder to communicate with outside agencies using PRINCE2. If a PRINCE2 term is shorthand for a concept, the champion may have to explain the concept in some detail before it will be adopted. An example would be Tolerance.

After some limited use of fragments of PRINCE2, the champion may gain credibility and be able to propose the overt implementation of PRINCE2.

The advantage of PRINCE2 by stealth is that it avoids time-consuming debates about the theoretical value of PRINCE2. Such debates can be particularly sterile when there has been a history of failed initiatives. It can be used as a proof of concept to help overcome prejudices or cynicism. Benefits will quickly arise from the adoption of some aspects of best practice in project management. On the other hand, PRINCE2 by stealth may result in a slow and partial implementation and higher maintenance of a modified vocabulary. Whether PRINCE2 by stealth is appropriate will depend on local circumstances.

4

STANDARDS, TEMPLATES AND TOOLS

This chapter looks at the impact of introducing standard environments for all the projects being undertaken by an organisation. These standard project environments fall short of a programme environment, as there will not be a single business vision. Nevertheless, there will be multiple projects that require some co-ordination, for example resource allocation. Such environments benefit the organisation, even though they may be less than optimal for each individual project.

4.1 The value of standards and templates

4.1.1 Cross-references to the PRINCE2 method

- Project Management team roles
  - Project Support
    - Project Support Office (PSO)

4.1.2 Example

An insurance company had to modify a large range of documents to comply with new regulations. Although the changes resulted in a significant amount of work for the IT department, they were of limited interest to the business as they would not generate additional revenue. Consequently, a programme was not created. Instead, a senior IT manager was given responsibility for co-ordinating a series of projects.

Various project management standards were already in place and complied with to varying extents. The IT manager, who was effectively acting as Senior Supplier on a number of Project Boards, enforced adoption of these standards. He persuaded the Project Boards to require standard Highlight Reports to be produced on a weekly basis. Indeed, he succeeded in creating a regime where Highlight Reports had to be created by a particular time each Monday. The existence of standard Highlight Reports allowed him to compare the status of his projects each Tuesday morning, in order to identify any actions that were needed.

4.1.3 Implementing

Organisations seek order and routine. Projects are unique, one-off, temporary management environments. PRINCE2 looks at the optimum management environment for any single project, therefore the management environment for each project will be different. Furthermore, the Project Management team, at the beginning of the project, will have to carry out the difficult task of designing that Project Management environment.

4.1.3.1 Advantages

Standards for managing projects offer three significant advantages:

- organisations prefer a degree of commonality across projects
- a standardised environment eases the task of designing the project environment at a time when the Project Management team is likely to be inexperienced
- PRINCE2 can be linked to other in-house standards.

Commonality of reporting across projects allows line managers, responsible for multiple projects, to quickly review each of their projects against common criteria. Consequently, the line manager, who is likely to also have a Project Board role on the projects in question, can quickly identify which projects need his or her attention.

If a Project Management team is inexperienced the processes of Start Up and Initiation can become elongated. The new team may draft and re-draft products such as the Project Brief and the Project Initiation Document as they come to grips with the underlying purpose of these documents. As time passes, circumstances will also evolve which will, in turn, trigger yet more changes in the draft documents. In the extreme, the project will never pass through DP2 (Authorising a Project). If this situation becomes endemic in an organisation, pressure may be brought to bear to start work before a Project Management environment is agreed. These difficulties can be avoided if local standards exist. Where there is an agreed local standard the newly formed Project Management team can have confidence in adopting the standard documentation and is likely to produce an acceptable product during the first draft.

Project standards can also cross-refer to other in-house standards such as ISO 9001, health and safety procedures or government regulations. Standards allow a Project Management environment to be agreed rapidly, before specialist work starts.

4.1.3.2 Disadvantages

Nevertheless, there are some associated disadvantages. In carrying out the survey that underpins this book, the greatest single criticism of PRINCE2 is that the method requires too many documents.

27

The PRINCE2 management product outlines do not indicate formats for management products. The structure within each project would be constrained to operate within a sub-optimal project management environment. Alternatively, the Project Management team might tailor the standard environment as implied by the standard project documentation. However, tailoring standards is little different from defining a one-off project management environment from scratch. Although it could be argued that a standard is a useful starter, there are likely to be additional barriers to gaining approval to modify standard templates.

The very term 'template' implies that a management product will be a stand-alone paper or electronic document. This is a false conclusion. If an organisation chooses to generate templates, it should also address those management products that will not routinely be created as stand-alone documents but will be combined with other management products, recorded informally or implemented verbally. For example, a procedure could emphasize that an Exception Report may be delivered verbally or by e-mail, but be produced in a particular timescale and communicated to all Project Board members at about the same time. Standard templates cannot precisely match individual projects. Therefore, the amount of detail in standard documentation is likely to be either too little or too great for each project.

When presented with a standard template there is much less ownership of underlying ideas than if they had been put together by the team from first principles. So, for example, if a standard template quotes Tolerance of +/-10%, the Project Management team is likely to adopt this figure without understanding the responsibilities of the Project Manager and Project Board that are implied by the concept of Tolerance.

There is also a tendency for a new Project Management team not just to use a standard document as a template, but also to copy it verbatim. This leads to a steady growth in the volume of text within standard documents and all of this text tends to be incorporated in the control documents for individual projects. The key information for a particular project becomes lost amidst this standard text. The reputation for bureaucracy is thus reinforced. Where this happens formally, the standard text can be regulated. However, there is a natural tendency, where templates exist, for standard text to be passed informally from one project to another. Thus if one Project Management team creates a crude but understandable piece of text describing, say, Configuration Management, this text will be copied on subsequent projects even though it may be inappropriate and possibly incorrect.

Over time, these factors tend to diminish the value of templates. Responsibilities should be allocated for the maintenance of templates, and documents scrutinised rigorously once drafted. The Project Management team is likely to be too close to documents to be able to carry out this rigorous scrutiny. Therefore, the question then is, who should carry out the scrutiny?

4.1.3.3 Conclusion

Well-designed and targeted templates and standards can ease the implementation of PRINCE2, while poorly thought through templates can slow the pace of projects and reinforce bad habits.

Templates and standards should only be introduced as part of a comprehensive implementation strategy, and to meet explicitly stated needs. Their maintenance should be considered before they are introduced. Furthermore, the use of standard text should be restricted and carefully monitored.

The PRINCE2 product outlines are readily available (from the PRINCE2 CD or at www.ogc.gov.uk/prince/onlineindex.htm) and are consistent templates. They can be implemented locally at a very low cost.

4.2 The role of the Project Support Office

4.2.1 Cross-reference to the PRINCE2 method

- Project Support Offices within the Project Management team roles appendix

4.2.2 Example

A Project Support Office (PSO) recruited a senior manager. He took to checking draft project documentation while Project Support staff were preparing it, before it had been returned to the Project Manager. If the Project Support Office manager was unhappy with the documentation he would instruct the Project Manager to amend it or threaten to report the matter to the Project Board. The Support Office manager had crossed the boundary from supporting the Project Manager to undermining his or her position.

4.2.3 Background

In terms of the balance of power within a project, the PRINCE2 manual is explicit in bounding the role of Project Assurance using phrases such as 'applicable standards are being used' and 'adherence to Quality Assurance standards'. The Project Manager's responsibilities are much broader, for example: 'The Project Manager's prime responsibility is to ensure that the project produces the required products, to the required standard of quality and within the specified constraints of time and cost. The Project Manager is also responsible for the project producing a result that is capable of achieving the benefits defined in the Business Case.' On balance, the Project Manager is accountable for managing the project.

However, within line organisations, the dominant power often lies with the permanent management structure – the PSO; not the temporary structure – the project. Consequently, this book takes a neutral stance on the power balance. It tacitly accepts the built-in advantage of permanent line structures in some cultures, which goes against the method as stated in the manual. To remain true to, and to carry forward the balance in, the manual, this book must consolidate the position described in PRINCE2. It is also worth recalling that PRINCE2 separates Project Assurance and Support. This separation reinforces the pivotal role of the Project Manager.

4.2.4 Implementing

A Project Support Office provides two functions:

- project administration services
- assistance with the efficient use of PRINCE2 standards.

A project is a temporary management environment, thus there will not be any administrative services in place within the project management environment when it is initially created. If resources are not provided to carry out this administrative effort Project Managers are forced to undertake this work themselves. This may be an inefficient use of a valuable resource. If these services can be centralised in a Project Support Office more efficient use will be made of scarce resources.

A Project Support Office can evolve as a centre of expertise for the use of planning tools and other aspects of project management. A Project Support Office is well positioned to be the custodians of templates. If a Project Support Office goes further by providing advice on the use of these templates then the Project Support Office becomes a repository for PRINCE2 expertise. It is then a small step for the Project Support Office to scrutinise completed templates.

This can cause problems. Project Managers are empowered to deliver projects on behalf of the Project Board acting as a body. If Support Office Managers intervene in this relationship, even if it is on behalf of one member of the Board, the authority of the Project Manager can be undermined.

The Project Support Office should help, assist or advise the Project Manager. The Project Support function must be subservient to the Project Manager if the Project Manager is to remain accountable for the day-to-day management of the project. A Project Support Office must, therefore, fulfil a matrix of responsibilities. Project Support Office staff will be accountable to the Project Manager for project information. They will also be administered by the Project Support Office manager.

Difficulties do emerge when Project Support Office staff begin to judge a Project Manager. So, for example, if PSO staff feel that a Project Initiation Document, based on a template owned by the Project Support Office, is inappropriate, they should rightly advise the Project Manager. The PRINCE2 method does not include a mechanism for any Project Support Office staff to pass on their dissenting view to other members of the Project Management team. If, however, the Project Manager chooses to reject the advice of the Project Support Office staff there is no mechanism within PRINCE2 for the Project Support Office staff to bypass the Project Manager and report the dissenting comments to the Project Board. Their only route for escalation is to raise a Project Issue.

Responsibility for confirming adherence to standards is, on the other hand, a Project Assurance responsibility. When PRINCE2 was created from PRINCE the functions of Project Assurance and Project Support were separated. This was because there was a conflict of interest between the Project Assurance function – monitoring the project on behalf of the Project Board; and the Project Support function – acting in support of the Project Manager.

Project Support Offices do still exist that combine these two functions. The combination of functions gives Project Assurance faster and wider access to project data from Project Support than from the Project Manager. Therefore, this combination of functions can undermine the clear accountability of the Project Manager. Combination of Project Assurance and Project Support functions is often attractive to a line culture. However, if this combination of functions is being considered, thought should be given to the diluting effect on the empowerment of Project Managers and, therefore, on projects.

4.2.4.1 Conclusion

The conclusion would seem to be that Project Support Offices are correctly positioned to maintain templates, but should not be given responsibility for checking the content of documents derived from templates unless the separation between the Project Assurance and Project Support functions has been established.

4.3 Tools

4.3.1 Cross-reference to the PRINCE2 method

- None

4.3.2 Example

A newly formed systems development company adopted PRINCE2 as a means of ensuring there was a standard approach to projects at a time of rapid growth. The company wished to improve co-ordination between projects so they chose to achieve this by standardising the format of plans between projects. They purchased a well-known scheduling tool and attempted to create a central repository of Project Plans that could be accessed by both the Project Support Office and Project Managers. The company expanded from a handful of staff to several hundred within less than a year. However, by the end of this period they had not managed successfully to implement the centralised scheduling tool. Project Managers were still maintaining their own project schedules using a variety of media.

Valuable effort had been wasted on trying to implement a sophisticated means of cross-project co-ordination. A more pragmatic solution, based on the principles of Management by Exception and Highlight Reporting, could have delivered the benefits associated with improved co-ordination. The format of Highlight Reports could have been standardised across projects, allowing Highlight Reports to be exchanged and compared. Projects could have remained free to produce plans in whatever format was felt to be appropriate for each project.

4.3.3 Implementing

There is strong demand for software to support project management in general and PRINCE2 in particular. These packages can be grouped into four categories:

- scheduling tools
- product-based planning tools
- document management tools
- Risk and Configuration Management tools.

4.3.3.1 Scheduling tools

There are numerous scheduling tools on the market and many seem to suggest that scheduling is a major element of project management. In comparison, PRINCE2 relegates scheduling to one process within Planning (PL5), which in turn is carried out during project initiation at each Stage Boundary (including before the initiation stage and when producing Team Plans). The PRINCE2 view is, therefore, that while scheduling tools are a useful adjunct for the Project Manager, they do not form the core of a project management system.

There is also a more fundamental concern for the PRINCE2 champion about scheduling tools. Scheduling tools imply that the complete plan for a project can be held as a single document. With the concepts of Levels of Plan and Management by Exception, PRINCE2 is more amenable to a view that each level within the Project Management team has limited visibility of plans at the next level of detail. So, for example, the Project Board will scrutinise a Stage Plan during Authorising a Stage or Exception Plan (DP3). The Project Manager is then empowered to execute that plan and to self-authorise plan deviations that are within Tolerance, as a result of Reviewing Stage Status (CS5). The Project Manager need only report the highlights of this amended Stage Plan to the Project Board (Reporting Highlights (CS6)). The Project Manager does not have to report all changes to a Stage Plan to the Project Board. Therefore, it can be argued that a Project Board does not need routine access to the details of a Stage Plan once they have approved it. Scheduling tools tend to assume that Project Board members want and need automatic visibility of Stage Plans. This seems to go against the concept of Management by Exception.

4.3.3.2 Product-based planning tools

The PRINCE2 view is that the product-based planning tools complement scheduling tools. These tools are discussed fully in Section 10.1, *Product-based planning.*

4.3.3.3 Document management tools

There are a number of tools on the market that offer:

- a summary of the PRINCE2 method
- electronic templates
- document-handling facilities.

The PRINCE2 manual is available electronically and contains an authoritative version of its method plus electronic templates, albeit with limited formatting and no customisation to local styles.

Competing products that are available offer summaries of the PRINCE2 method, which may not be authoritative. It is very difficult for any summary of something as complex and detailed as the PRINCE2 method to avoid altering its meaning. When summarising the method, these tools all tend to deviate from PRINCE2. Sometimes this deviation is small and unimportant, but these deviations could lead to confusion.

The tools also tend to contain templates that lack sound formatting. These templates cannot, by definition, be tailored to local culture without customising the software package. If these tools offer document handling it is usually within an electronic environment that is constrained within the software package. There are, therefore, likely to be difficulties when staff, who do not have access to the software package, attempt to manipulate these documents.

PRINCE2 document management tools would therefore seem to offer few advantages over the electronic manual and, indeed, might offer significant disadvantages.

4.3.3.4 Risk and configuration management tools

There are also a variety of sophisticated risk and configuration management tools on the market. These can be used effectively within a PRINCE2 environment. But effective risk management can be introduced without the use of specialist tools. The effort required to introduce and integrate specialist tools can sometimes divert management focus from other aspects of project management. The case for configuration management tools is stronger where there are complex configurations to be controlled. In these circumstances, there may already be tools in use in a parent organisation that provide a configuration management function, even if they are not referred to as configuration management tools.

4.3.3.5 Conclusion

Investigation of tools can be a time-consuming exercise that distracts the PRINCE2 champion from implementing the method effectively. Nevertheless, it is for the PRINCE2 champion to judge if these tools are of benefit.

5
MATURING PRINCE2

This chapter discusses the typical way in which an organisation becomes more mature in its use of PRINCE2.

Implementing PRINCE2 is not an overnight exercise. It takes time for an organisation to become comfortable with the use of the method. During an ordered implementation, existing projects will continue to use traditional standards while selected new projects will adopt PRINCE2. In a mature PRINCE2 organisation, PRINCE2 terms and concepts are perceived to be familiar and comforting, part of 'the way we do things around here'. However, in an organisation just starting to introduce PRINCE2, it is important to realise that it is much more straightforward to use the method on a project from the beginning than to apply PRINCE2 retrospectively.

The first PRINCE2 projects should be regarded as pilots. They should be large enough to justify a significant expenditure on project management but small enough to demonstrate quickly the value of PRINCE2. Care should be taken to ensure that they are properly resourced. Internal staff are likely to be unfamiliar with PRINCE2 and may therefore take longer to use PRINCE2 elements. This additional effort should be allowed for in estimates of the Project Management resource that will be required. It may also be appropriate to support the Project Management team for this part of the project with external PRINCE2 expertise. When pilot projects are being assessed, a false conclusion – that PRINCE2 involves a Project Management overhead – may be drawn. The correct conclusion, however, is that project management effort should reduce as staff gain experience of PRINCE2.

When an organisation first decides to use PRINCE2 it will have to make certain compromises in its project management environments. These compromises will be necessary given the existing culture and the experience of staff. As the background culture evolves and staff experience builds, organisations can make effective use of more of the PRINCE2 capability.

Organisations rarely make an explicit decision to introduce PRINCE2 incrementally. Incremental introduction occurs when inexperienced Project Management teams either choose not to adopt elements of PRINCE2 or pay lip service to elements but do not make effective use of them. By studying or assessing incremental introduction, the PRINCE2 champion may then appreciate why some elements of PRINCE2 are acceptable while others face resistance.

The evolutionary implementation of PRINCE2 tends to follow a predictable pattern. While this pattern will vary from site to site, some common themes emerge. Initially, project organisation is adopted with much emphasis on roles and responsibilities. Then template management products are introduced. With increasing confidence, a Controlled Start to projects becomes apparent. Next may come a quality-centred approach to planning and control, followed by the adoption of Management Stages and Management by Exception. Finally an organisation might tackle Product-Based Planning.

Incremental introduction can offer many advantages. It is perfectly valid to first tackle areas that provide the most useful added value, or to implement PRINCE2 in one specific area or for one project type. Such a partial implementation of PRINCE2 can act as a powerful proof of concept, convincing doubters and building support for a more comprehensive adoption of PRINCE2.

5.1 Project Organisation

5.1.1 Cross-references to the PRINCE2 method

- Organisation component
- Project Management team roles

5.1.2 Scaling

A limited introduction of PRINCE2 is more likely to occur where there is an external requirement to adopt the method. If there is little local interest in project management, the implementation of PRINCE2 may be reduced to the adoption of a set of job titles. The notion that project management can be reduced to the adoption of a new set of job titles is often attractive. A new set of job titles is high profile: meetings of the Project Board can be widely advertised, being visible in diaries, agendas and minutes.

There are few, if any, circumstances where it would be justifiable to scale PRINCE2 down to the use of job titles for the Project Management team without the adoption of the associated roles and responsibilities. In adopting PRINCE2, such a situation may be acceptable, however, as an initial first step. Business cultures can understand the Organisation component of PRINCE2. Managers only need to accept that projects are different, and therefore that they must exercise a different set of responsibilities when operating in a project environment than those responsibilities they exercise day to day.

5.1.3 Implementing

The weakness of this initial stage in the deployment of PRINCE2 is that managers involved are unlikely to understand the responsibilities that go with the job titles. Typically, although the job titles are adopted, managers continue to operate in their traditional ways. So, for example, the Project Management team roles may be interpreted to allow a hierarchy of managers to appear to be contributing to a project rather than actually functioning as key stakeholders. In addition, it is unlikely that Management by Exception will be operated in a manner that is any different from traditional ways of working in the background culture.

In such circumstances, Project Managers are unlikely to be empowered. They may feel they have been instructed to carry out the project without any resources being allocated to their day-to-day control. They may feel they have no communication channel with the Project Board. When they do meet with the Project Board, they may feel inhibited from entering into an open dialogue with the Board because of cultural constraints. Therefore, they may feel that PRINCE2 is not improving the lot of Project Managers.

Faced with these circumstances, the PRINCE2 champion has an evangelising role. He or she should encourage Project Managers to adopt those elements of PRINCE2 that are within their power. An example would be the creation of Work Packages for the teams under the control of the Project Manager. The PRINCE2 champion should also explain to practitioners that roles and responsibilities ideally need to be agreed at Start Up and during Initiation. It is unlikely that a significant rearrangement of roles and responsibilities can be undertaken at a Stage Boundary unless there has been a major crisis within the project. Therefore, the message to the Project Manager is that if he or she seeks a more appropriate Project Management environment, it must be negotiated at the beginning of the next project.

Finally, the PRINCE2 champion must attempt to gain access to the Project Board in order to explain to it that PRINCE2 is about more than the adoption of a set of job titles. It involves fundamental concepts such as Management by Exception, Quality-Centred and Product-Based Planning, and Management Stages. A positive way of achieving this is by first engaging the Project Board in the formulation of roles and responsibilities. This can be extended to the creation of a Project Initiation Document and then the inclusion of risk management or controls. Each element should only be introduced as the need for it becomes apparent.

Perhaps the most important requirement at this point in the adoption of PRINCE2 is to ensure that the initiative does not stall after the project job titles have been introduced. This phase has to be regarded as an initial and short-term step along the road to adopting PRINCE2.

New job titles may be the first timid steps towards adopting a new way of working. The PRINCE2 champion at least has an identified audience to whom he or she can present the advantages of PRINCE2.

5.2 Template management products

5.2.1 Cross-reference to the PRINCE2 method

- Management product outlines

5.2.2 Example

A government agency was formed by combining numerous existing departments. Much effort was put into defining a house style. Within the IT department there was considerable factional rivalry. One camp adopted PRINCE2 and commissioned a well-known management consultancy to implement the method. They did so, subsequently, by doing no more than introducing a set of templates. In this hierarchical organisation, use of the templates was imposed from above. Whenever a document was created from one of these templates the file properties showed the document to be owned by the management consultancy and the author to be one of the management consultants. In the absence of any other training in the method, the templates and PRINCE2 quickly fell into disrepute.

5.2.3 Implementing

Another early step in the introduction of PRINCE2 is the creation of standard templates. The pros and cons of standard templates in general terms are discussed in Chapter 4, *Standards, templates and tools.*

During the initial stages of the adoption of PRINCE2, templates can be seen as a further attempt to reinforce parallels between project and line management. The same approach underlies the early adoption of Project Management team job titles. In a process-orientated line culture, rules are codified into procedures that are published as documents. They may now be published via an intranet but still represent an attempt to delegate authority by codifying decision-making.

5.2.3.1 Disadvantages

To some extent the significance of templates have been heightened by management consultancies. A set of templates is a clear deliverable from a consultancy assignment. The consultancy may have to devote little effort to introducing existing templates to a new site. The client can quickly demonstrate results. The effect can be the creation of a large set of inappropriate templates that are not understood by project practitioners. The introduction of templates can, in fact, replace the education of project practitioners. The latter may be more useful.

The weakness of templates is that they are a poor mechanism for reflecting the temporary nature of a project management environment. They can work against tailoring and intelligent implementation. If difficult to amend, they reinforce an aura of bureaucracy.

Whereas a line process will be refined during development in order to be executed repeatedly, a Project Management environment will be defined once per project and only used once, within the project. Therefore, a perfect Project Management template would contain just two words: 'Use PRINCE2'.

5.2.3.2 Advantages

Templates do offer significant advantages during the implementation of PRINCE2 if they are used to form a bridge between the project and line cultures.

Staff can perceive PRINCE2 as an external threat. This fear of the unknown can be reduced if templates are created that reflect the house style. It should be easier for the new practitioner to use the correct template than to use any other source document. Therefore, the practitioner's word processing system should be set up to point to the new templates.

During the introduction of templates, attention should be paid to the look and feel of the templates. They should incorporate company logos, although care should be taken to ensure that the size of electronic templates does not, in consequence, grow. The templates should also be produced in the house font and incorporate house styles. It is even important to check that document properties show that the template is owned by the line organisation and not by some external agency. A consistent look and feel helps users anticipate what to expect and to interpret templates quickly.

There will be linkages between project and line cultures and the templates should be adjusted to accommodate these. For example, the PRINCE2 management product outline for a Business Case is very brief. A well-implemented template for a Business Case should contain links to an organisation's financial regulations for obtaining financial approval.

If an organisation does not wish to invest the time and effort into developing templates such as those described above, a simple and cheap solution is to purchase an electronic copy of the PRINCE2 manual. The content of management product outlines can then be copied for use as templates.

5.3 Controlled Start

5.3.1 Cross-references to the PRINCE2 method

- Starting Up a Project process
- Initiating a Project process
- Controlled Start element of Controls component

5.3.2 Example

During the Controlled Start of a pilot PRINCE2 project the Project Board were disappointed when, on completion of Authorising Initiation (DP1), they discovered that they would need to meet a second time to Authorise the Project (DP2). Expectations should have been set that it is perfectly reasonable for the Project Board to meet with the Project Manager on more that one occasion (DP1 and DP2).

5.3.3 Scaling

Having mastered the PRINCE2 Organisation component and generated internal templates, the next step for the organisation adopting PRINCE2 is to attempt the Controlled Start of new projects.

5.3.4 Implementing

Controlled Start is an interaction between the Project Manager and those senior managers who will become the Project Board. It is important at this point that the Project Management environment is agreed. As a result of Stage Selection, the routine interactions between the Project Manager and Project Board during the life of the project are also defined.

An organisation's first attempt at Controlled Start will result in PRINCE2 coming into close contact with existing organisational standards and practices. It is difficult to plot a pragmatic middle course during the Controlled Start of pilot projects. At one extreme, there might be an overly prescriptive implementation of PRINCE2. This could reinforce the stereotype of PRINCE2 as bureaucratic. At the other extreme, elements of PRINCE2 may simply be dropped because the organisation is likely to find it difficult to grasp all the concepts under-lying the PRINCE2 components. When PRINCE2 components are exposed to existing standards and practices, it is all too easy for the inexperienced PRINCE2 practitioner to regard the existing standards as a threat. A confrontational approach can easily emerge.

At this early point in the implementation of structured project management, the supporters of PRINCE2 should adopt a pragmatic approach. For the time being, it is much more important to build alliances and implement those parts of the method that can be introduced without causing conflict. For example, an existing set of procedures for moving software from a development to a live environment is the equivalent of part of a PRINCE2 Configuration Management method.

The correct tactic is to recognise where existing standards match PRINCE2 and incorporate those existing standards as part of the local implementation of PRINCE2.

During the first Controlled Starts, many templates and informal management products can be trialled. It is also acceptable for Start Up and Initiation to be combined, as described in the manual.

5.4 Quality-centred planning and control

5.4.1 Cross-references to the PRINCE2 method

- Quality component
- Product-Based Planning and Product Descriptions
- Initiating a Project process

5.4.2 Example

A consultant persuaded a site to adopt a quality-centred approach by arranging for Project Managers to produce Product Checklists. These Product Checklists were also used as Quality Logs. Introduction of just these two documents proved to be sufficient to maintain the required quality-centred approach.

5.4.3 Scaling

'Planning Quality (IP1) precedes Planning a Project (IP2).' This superficially simple statement within PRINCE2 reveals a fundamental aspect of the method. Quality Expectations, Acceptance Criteria and quality methods must all be agreed before the project is planned. During project planning, detailed analysis of quality requirements will be carried out as part of the production of Product Descriptions. This should be done during Identifying Activities and Dependencies (PL2), but before activities are defined or scheduled. In other words, quality comes first within a PRINCE2 project.

Quality planning must be carried out in an abstract environment, without detailed Project Plans. Furthermore, this quality-centred approach will also be carried through into monitoring progress. Monitoring the fitness for purpose of products ahead of monitoring the expenditure of time and effort is a difficult paradigm shift for many Project Managers. Traditionally, project practitioners first plan a sequence of work and then consider the quality checks to be carried out on products. As the implementation of PRINCE2 moves on, organisations must come to terms with the reversal in sequence that is inherent in planning quality before planning a project. This means an organisation must first understand the concepts of quality. For example, many organisations still equate the word 'quality' with 'excellence', rather than 'fitness for purpose'. A maturing organisation must delay project planning until after quality planning has been completed.

5.4.4 Implementing

When an organisation has successfully implemented templates and carried out the Controlled Start of a number of pilots it can be disheartening for them to be exposed to yet another new set of concepts. Consequently, many PRINCE2 implementations stall at this point. Organisational roles, templates and Controlled Start are used but the remaining elements of PRINCE2 are not implemented.

A simple, elegant, yet effective way of introducing the quality-centred approach is to encourage the use of Product Checklists during planning and control. As the Product Checklist includes a planned date for quality checks, these must be identified early in planning. For many projects, adequate Product Checklists can be produced without making use of product-based planning. When Checkpoint and Highlight Reports are generated, completed Product Checklists should be enclosed. A completed Product Checklist can be considered to be a simplified version of a Quality Log and, in many circumstances, the two management products can be combined.

Senior managers may resist seeing such a detailed document being presented as an attachment to a Highlight Report. It can be explained to them that they need not monitor the Product Checklist in detail. Its presence as part of a Highlight Report will reassure senior management that it is being completed conscientiously within the project.

An additional advantage of the use of Product Checklists is that the same document would be used as the basis for progress reporting at all levels within the project.

5.5 Stages and Exceptions

5.5.1 Cross-references to the PRINCE2 method

- Stages component
- Controls component – Management by Exception

5.5.2 Example

A newly trained PRINCE2 practitioner was running a project at a regional office on behalf of the company headquarters. The Project Board was at a senior level and was initially reluctant to receive communication directly from the fairly junior Project Manager.

The Project Manager had previously sought guidance from the Project Board on a particular Issue, but no response had been forthcoming. He therefore raised an Exception Report stating that, in the absence of a response from the Project Board, he would release the project team members back to their parent organisations at the end of the week. Within minutes, he received a phone call from the Executive on the Project Board. The Project Manager found himself in the Executive's office at nine o'clock the following morning. The Project Manager had had to travel the length of the country overnight, but had succeeded in gaining the attention of the Project Board, albeit in a rather dramatic way.

5.5.3 Implementing

Time-based management reporting seems to be the norm across many industry sectors. It may occur as frequently as weekly or as rarely as annually. If any event-based reporting exists, it is likely to be linked to the end of technical stages. Reporting usually takes the form of some type of summary of progress. Again, there can be wide variation in terms of format, which may range from informal to narrative-based, and in levels of delegation. These two concepts, time-based reporting and reporting by summary, are the antithesis of the PRINCE2 concepts of event-based Management by Exception.

Even on sites that appear to have fully integrated PRINCE2 into the culture, event-based Management by Exception may still be missing. A change to event-based Management by Exception requires a Project Board to adjust its preferred management style. This can often be difficult to achieve. Consequently, the advantages of Management by Exception in terms of reducing the reporting workload and the power of this decision-making tool can be lost.

Where projects consist of an initiation stage and only one other stage, a limited implementation of PRINCE2 only comes to the fore when projects go into Exception. However, where projects are larger or more risky, and therefore involve a number of stages, many of the benefits of PRINCE2 will be lost if event-based Management by Exception is not used.

The options for the PRINCE2 champion are to explain proactively the advantages of Management by Exception, or reactively to manoeuvre the Project Board to Manage by Exception when an appropriate event arises. The champion should attempt to be proactive and explain the concepts of Management by Exception during Start Up or Project Board training. If the champion is a member of the Project Board, or can gain the support of one of the Board's members, this is much easier to achieve. However, the champion should not be surprised if he or she is less than successful. The only opportunity the champion may then have to encourage Management by Exception might be when the project exceeds Tolerance. In preparation, all the PRINCE2 champion can do is ensure that Stage Plans are sufficiently light that they can easily be updated should a project go into Exception. The starting point is to create an Exception Report, which of course does not need to be a written document. The Exception Report should clearly put the onus on the Project Board to take a decision.

The PRINCE2 Exception mechanism is an effective way of bringing a project back under control. Therefore, the value of Management by Exception is best demonstrated to senior management by showing its effectiveness in practice.

The PRINCE2 champion may not succeed at first. He or she will be unproven and Project Board members inexperienced. In a blame culture, this can be a difficult period for the PRINCE2 champion. At times, Project Managers have to be courageous, as the benefits of effective Management by Exception are significant.

5.6 Product-based planning

5.6.1 Cross-reference to the PRINCE2 method

- Product-Based Planning techniques

5.6.2 Example

A PRINCE2 site was out of the habit of using product-based planning techniques during project planning. They had a particularly time-critical project to undertake over the following year, so they used an external facilitator to conduct a product-based planning workshop. During the workshop the members of the team identified an additional four months of effort which, at that point in the project, could be accommodated. However, had the product-based planning techniques not been used the project is likely to have missed its deadline.

5.6.3 Scaling

If an organisation has already implemented the elements of PRINCE2 previously described in this chapter – organisational roles, templates, Controlled Start, quality-centred planning and control, and stages and exceptions – it is likely to have an effective PRINCE2 environment. Most other elements of PRINCE2 are also likely to have been adopted along the way. Nevertheless, there may still be a reluctance to make full use of product-based planning.

By now, Product Descriptions are likely to be in use, but it is fairly common for Product Breakdown Structures and Product Flow Diagrams not to be in evidence. One reason for this is that the only known product-based planning tool is dated and operates in an enclosed environment. In other words, Product Flow Diagrams, Product Descriptions and Product Breakdown Structures contained within the tool are held and manipulated within the package and cannot easily be accessed from within other software. Links can be created, but organisations are often reluctant to devote time to this work. Therefore, PRINCE2 practitioners feel there is a shortage of product-based planning support tools.

There is also likely to be a distinct shortage of product-based planning skills. Breakdown Structures and Flow Diagrams are only taught to a very basic level on most training courses. Staff emerge from training without the skills to use these tools effectively on a typical project. If every Project Manager attempts to create Breakdown Structures and Flow Diagrams, they will only do so every few months at best. Therefore, their basic skills are not reinforced.

There also tends to be a misunderstanding of the advantages of each of these two diagramming techniques. Product Breakdown Structures are useful general-purpose communication tools; and the Product Flow Diagram is of greatest assistance in projects where there are complex dependencies. Many PRINCE2 practitioners do not differentiate between the two techniques.

This combination of limited IT support, a failure to differentiate between techniques and, most importantly, inadequate skills results in neither Product Breakdown Structures nor Product Flow Diagrams being adopted.

5.6.4 Implementing

The way round these issues is to encourage the incremental adoption of product-based planning techniques in appropriate circumstances.

Project Managers should be encouraged, as an interim step, to use Breakdown Structures without tackling Flow Diagrams. Breakdown Structures can be drawn in presentation packages, which are likely to be widely available and understood. There is also no need to maintain the product-based view of the project throughout its duration. The first iteration Product Breakdown Structure can be created at the beginning of a project and used as an input to a Gantt chart. It can then be discarded and the project managed using the Gantt chart and a Product Checklist. The next step is to revisit the Product Breakdown Structure at Stage Boundaries, but again not to maintain both a Gantt chart and a Product Breakdown Structure during the stage.

A similar approach should be taken with Product Flow Diagrams. First, they should only be used on some projects, then they should only be created at the beginning of a project, and eventually they can be created at each Stage Boundary.

Project Support Office staff can assist with product-based planning for all projects and stages, and will rapidly build-up expertise. They are also well placed to support product-based planning packages.

An incremental approach will lead in the long run to more a more widespread adoption of product-based planning techniques.

6

SCALING – TYPES OF ORGANISATIONS AND PROJECTS

Before considering how users of PRINCE2 can scale down elements appropriately, it is useful to consider various characteristics of organisations and projects.

The factors covered in this chapter can apply to any project but will tend to be more significant when applied to smaller projects. At first sight, it might seem that small projects will be simpler to manage than large ones. It is certainly true that medium-sized projects are easier to manage than very large ones. However, as projects shrink down to a very small scale a new set of difficulties emerge. Therefore, in terms of project management, small projects can actually be more difficult than large projects.

This chapter focuses on the pitfalls that can be most apparent in small projects. For the purpose of this book, a small project would last less than six elapsed weeks and would have a budget of 20–30 person days of effort.

6.1 Types of organisations

Whereas the detailed impact of organisational cultures is covered under implementing PRINCE2, some broader characteristics of organisations affect how PRINCE2 is scaled.

6.1.1 Customer/Supplier environments

If a Customer/Supplier environment is commercial and there is a prime contractor or system integrator, someone from that company will be the Senior Supplier. If there is no prime contractor but a number of subcontractors, there will need to be either multiple Senior Suppliers or a Senior Supplier from the Customer. Each subcontractor is likely to provide at least one Team Manager. There may also be Customer and Supplier Project Assurance and a variety of other communication channels between and amongst contractors and the Customer.

If the Customer/Supplier environment is non-commercial, it is more appropriate to scale back certain aspects of PRINCE2. Notably the Project Management team can be simpler. It might be possible to do without Team Managers, and Project Assurance should be more straightforward. In the absence of Team Managers and contracts, the split between Controlling a Stage (CS) and Managing Product Delivery (MP) may become blurred.

6.1.2 Partnerships

In the absence of commercial relationships there may instead be partnerships. Typically, this can involve several public bodies working together to provide a linked service. Voluntary and independent bodies may also join such initiatives.

Arrangements catering for partnership can become extremely complex and involve a large number of agencies. Project Boards, for example, can have more than a dozen members. Typically, no one agency holds sway over the others, therefore a consensus has to be built on each decision. Large consensual Project Boards work very slowly and the pace of their projects is likely to suffer. Alternatively, Project Managers begin to take decisions that are beyond their remit. Consideration should then be given to adopting at least the organisational structures of programme management.

Such projects can also become large and of long duration. The PRINCE2 method is not explicit about the largest size for a project, but it is reasonable to consider using programme management techniques – such as a programme management organisation layer, stakeholder or benefit management – if project duration exceeds one year to 18 months or if project effort is greater than about 50–75 person years.

6.1.3 Deadline-based organisations

Many organisations work around fixed deadlines, for example government bodies that interact with elected members on a pre-defined cycle, schools, and the tourist industry.

When applying PRINCE2 in an environment with standing deadlines, the PRINCE2 champion has to align the end of management stages with these deadlines. Moreover, the end of any stage has to be far enough ahead of these deadlines so that any Stage Exceptions are likely to be dealt with before the deadline. At the very least, positive Stage Tolerance must run out before the fixed deadline. The lead-time for passing documents to any external bodies must also be allowed for. When taken together, actions to accommodate deadlines can compress and constrain the time available for specialist work.

6.2 Short durations

The first problem encountered by the manager of a small project is that the project is likely to be of short duration and hence have limited elapsed time contingency. The difficulty with such a project is that if there is a one-day delay – for example, in approving the Project Initiation Document – it could absorb a substantial amount of the contingency for the whole project. The conclusion is that the Project Manager on a small project must monitor any lag there may be between activities: for example, the time it takes to send a document from one office to another location; or periods of time when individuals are unavailable, even if only for a few hours.

Tolerance is the permissible deviation from a plan, a control mechanism. It serves the same purpose as that vaguer concept of contingency. Commonly, staff add contingency to estimates both to provide flexibility when controlling a project and as an allowance for risks such as task overruns. PRINCE2 separates these two allowances into Tolerance and a contingency allowance for specific risks. One might expect a small project to have a project Tolerance of less than three elapsed days (or 10% of the duration). To cater for limited flexibility over the timing of tasks, **one solution is to allow a larger time Tolerance on short projects.**

6.3 Diversions: full- and part-time teams

Project teams are brought together for the duration of a project and then return to their routine work. The manager of a small project is therefore more likely to find that staff are working on the project on a part-time basis. Even when staff are full-time on the project they will be subject to various absences. However, these absences are fairly predictable. They will of course be sick and have holidays, but allowances for all these absences should be built into estimates. They will also not be productive for eight hours a day every day. Again, this should be catered for in the estimating rules used by the Project or Team Manager.

Furthermore, some allowance should be made for contacts with the sections from which team staff came. Inevitably, project team members either have to contact colleagues they have previously worked with, or those colleagues will contact the team members. Once this contact has been made, it is very likely that the project team members will be diverted into providing various types of informal support for their old organisations. While this diverts them from their own project work, it does maintain communications with the outside world and helps to build goodwill. This again should be allowed for within the estimating rules.

When a project's team members are part-time, all these pressures still exist. Indeed, they are often of the same scale as they would be if team members were full-time. To take a simple example, it takes as long to phone a colleague if you are full-time on a project as when you are part-time. But the extent of the diversion as a percentage of the total effort that the part-time team member is expending on the project is significantly increased. A half-hour diversion in an eight-hour working day is manageable; a half-hour diversion for a person who is 25% on a project is half an hour in two hours.

The net result is that part-time team members suffer more absences and diversions then do full-time team members. This should be allowed for when Designing a Plan (PL1).

6.4 Parallel working

Part-time team members are inevitably working part-time on something else. This may be their normal work or it may be other small projects. Either way, their other work will fluctuate and they will have to manage conflicting priorities.

For simplicity, consider that part-time team members are working on a number of small projects. If they are diverted from a project, for whatever reason, they will fall behind with the work of that project. In order to catch up, they may work slightly less on one project and longer on another. Once again, a short diversion will be very significant if the practitioners only have part-time members for a percentage of their time. The net effect is that the Project Manager cannot rely on having part-time team members available to work on the project as consistently as full-time team members do. He or she also cannot rely on getting access to team members when required.

Variable availability becomes significant when activities are on a critical path. Either the Project Manager must negotiate guaranteed availability or introduce greater Tolerance. Both these actions should be taken in advance during Project or Stage Planning (IP2 or SB1).

6.5 Multiple concurrent projects

6.5.1 Disturbances

When disturbed in the middle of a task, a person has to deal with the disturbance and then re-familiarise him or herself with the original task. This effect applies to team members on every occasion that they stop and start work on a project. In the extreme, if individuals are tasked with working on too many projects – for example, those working part-time – they will simply stand still on all of the projects, expending a lot of effort but making no forward progress.

This effect is most noticeable in organisations with broad responsibilities. They may also require complex ways of judging the relative importance of the various aspects of their remit. This is often seen, for example, in government bodies with wide responsibilities.

Projects involving part-time working are considerably less efficient than projects involving full-time working. The solution is to undertake fewer projects in parallel or allocate staff full time to projects for limited periods.

6.5.2 Benefit realisation

Each individual project has a Business Case offering certain benefits if a particular amount of effort is expended. If an individual is working on multiple part-time projects, some of those projects will have better Business Cases than others. If an organisation attempts to move all the projects forward in parallel, projects with sound Business Cases may be delayed by projects with less sound Business Cases.

If programme management is not adopted, the organisation should clearly prioritise projects, putting on hold those with less sound Business Cases and progressing as rapidly as possible those that are more advantageous.

PRINCE2 helps prioritisation by putting the Business Case to the fore during Initiating a Project (IP) so that the Business Case is rigorously examined during Authorising a Project (DP2).

6.6 Irreducible costs

6.6.1 Scaling

There are often limitations on how many staff can work on a project. Therefore, small projects often have particularly small budgets.

As with diversions, some activities do not scale. For example, creating a Checkpoint Report takes a certain minimum amount of time, whether there are 10 products being produced or 100. In addition, there are certain minimum costs that have to be borne during each week of a project's existence. Therefore, there is a tendency for project management to occupy a larger percentage of the budget of a small rather than a large project.

This trend is exacerbated whenever problems arise. With experience, it is possible to use PRINCE2 for small projects but application of the method requires a lightness of touch. When a small project goes into Exception the Project Manager still needs to produce some sort of Exception Report (CS8) for the Project Board to give Ad Hoc Direction (DP4). The Project Manager must then produce a Project or Stage Exception Plan (SB) and the Project Board must Authorise the Plan (DP3). The minimum duration of each process might be only a few minutes, but inexperienced Project Managers find the task of carrying out a series of PRINCE2 steps in a short timescale, without missing out any vital elements, to be perhaps the most difficult aspect of scaling PRINCE2. To take this point to the extreme, even finding the relevant part in the PRINCE2 manual and reminding oneself of the underlying principles can take a significant amount of time.

Small projects may, therefore, not be suitable pilots for the introduction of PRINCE2. Furthermore, a part-time Project Manager on a small project is not a suitable role for an inexperienced Project Manager.

6.6.2 Example and cross-reference to the PRINCE2 method

A Project Board had scheduled an End Stage Assessment (DP3) for 5.30 p.m. one evening. The Executive was unable to attend and had asked one of her trusted colleagues, who was providing Project Assurance, to represent her. The rest of the Project Board was content with this arrangement.

At the meeting, the Project Assurance individual reported that he had discussed the results of quality checks with some of his colleagues before attending. He had discovered that insufficient attention had been paid to the implications of some proposed procedures. A risk had previously been identified that precisely these circumstances might arise. Consequently, it was agreed that the product (the new procedures) were not fit for purpose. As this product was the major product of the previous stage, it was agreed that the stage was now in Exception.

The Senior Supplier, a very experienced PRINCE2 practitioner, advised the Project Manager to make a verbal notification of an Exception Report (CS8). She did so immediately in a phone call to the Executive and it was agreed that the Project Board could meet at 8.30 a.m. the following morning, before several members of the Board attended a nine o'clock meeting.

At 8.15 a.m. the Project Manager and Senior Supplier convened to produce a verbal Exception Plan (SB). By 8.30 a.m. they were in a position to present the Exception Plan, again verbally, to the full Project Board, which had now convened in the foyer of the office block where the nine o'clock meeting would take place.

Following a brief discussion (DP3), it was agreed that the product that had been identified as being not fit for purpose would be added to the Stage Plan for the next stage, with some appropriate adjustment to the timescale and budget of the stage. The Project Board gave verbal authorisation to the Project Manager to modify the new Stage Plan and by nine o'clock the Mid-Stage Assessment had finished.

It had therefore taken 1.5 hours of working time for the project to go into and be recovered from Exception over a period of less than 16 elapsed hours. As some 13 processes had been executed, the conclusion is that PRINCE2 processes can be very short.

7

HOW TO SCALE

7.1 Introduction

When organisations first implement PRINCE2 they may be asked to explain their approach. Frequently they say that they did not need 'full PRINCE2' so they have only implemented portions of it. This can reveal a flawed understanding of the method. PRINCE2 is designed to be scalable, so scaling it appropriately *is* 'full PRINCE2'.

7.1.1 What scaling entails

Scaling does not consist of omitting elements of PRINCE2 for various reasons. PRINCE2 is not a series of isolated silos – each containing a technique, process or component – whereby any element can be omitted with no effect on the others. PRINCE2 is a web of interlinking elements. Components take place in processes; techniques are undertaken to bring to life components; individuals fulfilling project roles create management products. By looking at the concepts behind a component the practitioner can understand how to scale it without losing its value. Also, processes can be carried out informally, management products can be verbal, or elements of the method can be combined. That said, if the practitioner omits an element completely, the framework of PRINCE2 is weakened. **Scaling, therefore, comes down to using elements with a lightness of touch.**

7.1.2 Chapter content

This chapter looks at a variety of different approaches to simplifying or scaling PRINCE2, none of which involve omitting elements. One approach involves defining a minimum set of elements that must be present, in full, for a project to be considered a PRINCE2 project. Another approach is to consider various characteristics of a project and how these can be used to guide the practitioner when scaling. Some form of matrix or checklist can be created, relating project characteristics to relevant elements of PRINCE2. Both approaches can also be combined.

7.1.3 Cross-reference to the PRINCE2 method

- Applicable to the complete method

7.1.4 Example

Examples of a minimum set of PRINCE2 elements, or of specific guidance on how to scale PRINCE2 based on project characteristics, have not been included. Had they been included there would have been a risk that they might have been implemented without question. For the same reason, no example is quoted for this section. However, there are a number of local procedures that have been successfully implemented, giving guidance on how to apply PRINCE2.

Guidance on when to scale PRINCE2 must be site-specific and based on the characteristics of the projects involved and the line culture of the organisation.

7.1.5 Informality

7.1.5.1 Cross-reference to the PRINCE2 method

Appendix A to the PRINCE2 manual contains Product Description outlines of the standard management and quality products. The term 'Product Description outlines' rolls off the tongue of a trainer, but many practitioners fail to appreciate the significance of these.

First, they have similar contents as any product description. They are only 'outlines' because they omit both the format and the method by which the fitness for purpose of the management products will be checked. This information is unique to each project.

This section concentrates on the format – the look and feel – of management products, which applies to specialist products as well. It is the format of a product that changes when it is used informally. Look and feel can be stated in terms of quality criteria and be subject to sometimes quite detailed quality checks. But the format heading is intended to cover something different; it is intended to give the reader a picture of what the product will actually be like. Many assume that management products must be written documents. The method deliberately does not constrain the format of management and quality products.

7.1.5.2 Example

Just as PRINCE2 was being released a local authority implemented an in-house version of the method. They chose to publish a manual explaining it and recruited two experienced PRINCE practitioners to undertake the work.

The discussion turned to templates. The PRINCE experts had in mind electronic templates, to be used in the word processor package then being introduced on the site. The Project Manager envisaged typed paper templates that could be photocopied. Of course, both groups simply referred to these as templates and, when discussing the outline of the Product Descriptions, they were identical. The only difference between the two types of template – electronic and paper – was the format. After much confusion the team wrote Product Descriptions that revealed the differences between the two concepts and an agreement was reached. In fact, the local authority decided to produce both electronic and paper templates.

7.1.5.3 Scaling

When scaling PRINCE2, the Project Manager must consider the format of any management products they intend to use. Management products are created, typically, using a word processor. More informally, they can be created as e-mails, which are still filed electronically. They can also be in the format of telephone calls or meetings, with the details of a conversation or notes of the meeting simply being recorded as a note on the file.

At the other extreme, more sophisticated organisations have internal intranets or knowledge bases. Intranets are becoming increasingly popular, however a difficulty emerges if there is a commercial Customer/Supplier environment. There can be additional complexity if a secure extranet has to be implemented across a commercial relationship.

There are also a number of stand-alone products including management product templates and project management packages. Document management software is becoming increasingly common and offers many of the facilities needed to create and control management products. From a project viewpoint, the selection and implementation of such a project management package has to be justified within the timescale of the project. Using this hard criterion, it is difficult to justify such products. However, there may be justifiable reasons for applying common standards across projects. This point is considered in more detail in Chapter 4, *Standards, templates and tools.*

7.1.5.4 Implementing

Organisational culture is extremely important when considering the format of management products. Some sites react badly to documentation and are more comfortable with meetings, conversations and the occasional e-mail. This approach is perfectly suitable provided some records are maintained. Cultures that are more traditional tend to focus on meetings and minutes of those meetings. Traditional minutes may not be an effective vehicle for managing projects, however. They tend to focus effort on recording the status during the meeting and details of individual decisions. Consequently, they can inhibit the pace of a project. Some cultures also require records to be kept for auditing or regulatory purposes. The format(s) chosen need(s) to complement these requirements.

The main role of management products is to assist in running the project. Choosing an appropriate format is a balance between the effort required to create the product and the permanence of the product. The final choice depends on the background culture.

7.1.6 Combining

7.1.6.1 Cross-reference to the PRINCE2 method

- Applies to all components and management products

7.1.6.2 Example

A Senior Supplier received a mobile phone message saying that the project Executive had seen a report, which formed a major deliverable of the project, and wished to make certain changes. The caller, fulfilling a Project Assurance role on behalf of the Executive, wished to inform the Project Manager but did not wish to suggest that the Project Manager had been remiss in her responsibilities. The Project Manager came from the Supplier's organisation rather than the Customer's organisation (as is suggested in the PRINCE2 manual). The Senior Supplier contacted the Project Manager by mobile phone and they identified various options (CS8).

The 'do nothing' and 'delay the project' options were rejected. An alternative option was to delay a meeting of the Project Board so that the document could be reworked. This introduced a risk that the Project Board might wish to alter the document a second time. Elapsed time contingency had been written into the plan to allow for this possibility. This time would now be used for re-working the document. The Senior Supplier advised the Project Manager to adopt the third option. As it was more convenient, the Senior Supplier rang the Project Assurance person to propose the options. The Project Assurance person, the only individual not on a mobile phone, sent an e-mail to all concerned, which was the revised Stage Plan (SB). The combination of a number of processes meant it had taken less than one hour for the project to enter and be recovered from Exception.

7.1.6.3 Processes

Many who are new to PRINCE2 find it difficult to judge the typical scale of a process, which is a PRINCE2 term meaning some sort of event. Processes can range from a formal workshop that lasts for several days; a meeting lasting several hours; the production of a simple document, taking perhaps an hour to devise; an e-mail, a telephone conversation, or a passing comment in a corridor. Those new to PRINCE2 may find it useful to think of processes as lasting from half an hour to half a day.

7.1.6.3.1 Scaling

Having established the scale of an individual process there is scope for merging processes without necessarily omitting any of them. For example, within Initiating a Project (IP), Refining the Business Case and Risks are a single process (IP3) because both the

Business Case and the Risk Log will have been worked on recently. Within Managing Stage Boundaries (SP), Updating the Risk Log (SB4) and Updating the Business Case (SB3) are separate processes. The logic for this is that neither the Risk Log nor the Business Case may have been looked at for some considerable time, so there may be a need for each to be reviewed in some detail. In a project with short stages, and a straightforward Business Case and Risk Log, reviewing both these documents could take only a few minutes. Indeed, it may be perfectly reasonable for the review of these documents to be no more than a conversation. In this case, the two processes are actually being combined.

The example above takes scaling to the extreme – the whole of Managing Stage Boundaries (SB) was completed in a single telephone conversation. This is not recommended for most projects, but it can be appropriate in some circumstances.

7.1.6.3.2 Implementing

PRINCE2 process models have not yet become ingrained in the culture of many organisations. No doubt in time individual processes will become recognised as events in an organisational culture. The exception is meetings of Project Boards. Authorising a Stage or Exception Plan is recognised in many cultures as a meeting of the Project Board. If it is convened as a stand-alone meeting, managers clear time in their diaries and expect to spend several hours poring over a project.

An alternative approach is to combine the Project Board meeting with another frequent, routine meeting. This can help busy people with diary management. So, for example, if a line management team meets weekly, the Project Board meeting can occasionally be the final agenda item. There are advantages to changing the mood of the meeting by having some people leave while others join the meeting, which is easily arranged. The net effect is that Project Board meetings shrink from being several hours long to lasting only a few minutes. This encourages Project Boards to delegate the detail of the project to the Project Manager and to focus instead on the overall view of the project.

7.1.6.4 Management products

7.1.6.4.1 Scaling

The most widespread form of scaling PRINCE2 involves the simplification of PRINCE2 management products. Changing the format of individual management products has already been discussed, but **it is also possible to combine documents.** For example, a Project Mandate, Project Brief and Project Initiation Document could be combined into a single composite document. This would be appropriate if the Controlled Start of a project was straightforward and Starting Up a Project (SU) and Initiating a Project (IP) were combined.

There are many circumstances when reporting documents can be combined. If there is no Team Manager, the Quality Log, Checkpoint Report and Highlight Report can be combined. Or, at the end of a project the Lessons Learned Report, Follow-on Action Recommendations, End Project Report and Post-Project Review Plan could be combined into a single document.

When combining documents, the practitioner should take care to ensure that the full scope of the new, combined and therefore broader document is covered. Combined documents may also require a wider distribution and could compromise confidentiality. If confidentiality is to be maintained, the content in a combined document may have to be censored, thus reducing openness and honesty.

7.1.6.4.2 Implementing

It is easy to move to the next step: deciding to always combine documents. This decision is acceptable if an organisation always carries out similar projects. If there is variation in the type and size of projects, however, individual decisions on how to combine management products should be taken by the Project Management team. **If an organisation merely defines a new set of standard templates, there is a danger of them being overly rigorous for some projects and too light for others.** This aspect of implementing management products is also covered in Chapter 4.

7.2 Scaling methodologies

PRINCE2 is known as a methodology. However, the original definition of methodology – a study of methods – is inappropriate when applied to PRINCE2. The term has evolved within PRINCE2 to mean something more than a single technique; PRINCE2 is more a collection of elements. It is a complementary framework of processes, components and techniques. The art of implementing PRINCE2, therefore, is in choosing which of those elements to use and how rigorously to apply them.

Some sites choose to create a second methodology – a methodology for applying PRINCE2. Scaling methodologies tend to consist of a number of different approaches for deciding how rigorously PRINCE2 should be applied in particular circumstances. There are pitfalls associated with these scaling methodologies. They are yet another set of techniques to be developed, documented, taught, learnt, applied and maintained. Scaling methodologies have to be used at the beginning of a project when the learning curve for the Project Management team is steep and understanding of the characteristics of a particular project is at its lowest. Nevertheless, scaling methodologies are popular. Organisations implementing PRINCE2 may wish to make the choices associated with scaling the method structured, repeatable and straightforward for the new practitioner. So, the following sections look at several of the common scaling methods that have emerged. These can be broken down into:

- definition of a minimum set of elements that must be present
- guidance on how to scale, based on the project characteristics for a particular project.

Put simply, project characteristics can be as basic as size measured by time or cost. Or, they can be more sophisticated, involving an assessment of, for example, complexity, impact or risk. Guidance in how to scale processes, components and techniques is given in subsequent chapters.

7.3 A minimum set of PRINCE2 elements

There is a danger associated with defining a minimum set of elements for a project. If no advice is promulgated concerning when additional elements of PRINCE2 are required, there will be a tendency for only this minimum set to be used, even in circumstances where it would be appropriate to make use of other aspects of PRINCE2.

Without knowing the circumstances in a particular culture, this book cannot suggest an authoritative minimum set. This section is intended, however, to assist readers to define their own minimum set of PRINCE2 elements.

7.3.1 Controlled Start – an initiation stage

Any PRINCE2 project should have some form of Initiation Stage, which may consist of a combination of the Start Up and Initiation processes. During this stage all of the following components should be considered, however briefly.

7.3.1.1 Business Case

The justification for undertaking a project should be noted, in terms that are familiar to the Customer organisation. A statement of cost, again in terms that are recognisable within the culture, should also be proffered. If any category of costs (for example, internal staff time) is not recorded then these costs will not be controllable.

7.3.1.2 Organisation

There should be some statement concerning responsibilities for the project. At an absolute minimum, the person responsible for day-to-day control – the Project Manager – and the individual or group committing resources to the project – the Project Board – should be nominated.

7.3.1.3 Quality

The criteria against which the final product, at least, will be checked should be recorded. A statement should also be made about how fitness for purpose will be judged. The terminology surrounding the Quality component can be quite complex. Stripping away the terminology, a view should be expressed on what will be acceptable.

7.3.1.4 Plans

Some form of statement of intent concerning how products will be created should be recorded. This need not be a diagram but it is likely to consist of more than just a simple chart. A site may wish to specify that all the components of a Plan should be included, however briefly (see the diagram in the Plans component of the PRINCE2 manual). Whilst it is acceptable for a Plan to focus on activities and resources, there should be some mention of at least one product to ensure that the project focuses on the outcome, not just the business of the project.

7.3.1.5 Controls

How monitoring and control will be carried out should be stated. Such a statement should include the formality, frequency and content of reporting. The items to be reported on should also be noted. Typically, these would include but not be limited to:

- the fitness for purpose of products
- progress against time and budget
- Business Case viability
- the unexpected, i.e. Issues, risks, etc.

There should also be some indication of the discretion, that is the Tolerance, delegated to the Project Manager.

7.3.1.6 Management of risk

Associated with the definition of controls should be some indication about how the adverse consequences of future events, risk, will be handled. In addition, there should be a list of risks and some statement concerning the current view on the likelihood of risks occurring.

7.3.1.7 Stages

As a small, low-risk project is likely to have only one stage, other than the initiation stage, then there need be no explicit reference to stages.

7.3.1.8 Configuration Management

A statement should be made about how products will be safeguarded. This may be as simple as stating who will be responsible for this process and, therefore by implication, for defining and controlling versions. This individual will, in effect, be the Configuration Librarian. In addition, a statement should be made about how and where items will be filed – the Project File.

7.3.1.9 Change Control

How changes will be assessed and authorised should also be noted. This could even be a statement that a mechanism will only be defined if any changes are raised.

7.3.1.10 Project Initiation Document

The conclusions reached following Initiation should be recorded in some format. A conversation may be acceptable, however it is more likely that a culture will insist that these conclusions are recorded in some form of document. It is also prudent for all those involved, particularly the Project Manager, to have a record of what has been agreed to prevent future misunderstandings.

The items to be covered above have been described in about 500 words, and can be accommodated on a single, typed page of A4. A Project Initiation Document could be equally small: at a minimum, covering only one or two pages. Some authorised individual or group – the Project Board – should approve the Project Initiation Document.

7.3.2 Controlled Progress

7.3.2.1 Plans

During the execution of a project there should be access to some form of Plan. This Plan should be updated only as frequently as is necessary to allow control to be exercised, in accordance with the Project Initiation Document. As has been mentioned, the final product at least should be defined in this Plan.

7.3.2.2 Review

Some mechanism for checking products should be exercised and the result(s) of this check(s) should be noted in accordance with the Quality and Configuration Management portion of the Project Initiation Document.

7.3.2.3 Reporting

Reports should be made as defined in the Project Initiation Document. Again, it is worth noting that these may be verbal in certain circumstances. Management by Exception will be in operation so these reports are likely to be brief.

7.3.3 Controlled Close

At the end of the project the Project Manager should notify its completion to the responsible individual or group: the Project Board. As well as stating that the Project has finished, the Project Manager's report should cover:

- products that have been accepted
- support arrangements
- any lessons to be learned
- how realisation of the Business Case will be measured.

7.3.4 Techniques

As noted above, the Plan should include at least one product, the means of filing, the means of checking (Quality Reviews) and a way of capturing changes.

7.4 Types of guidance on how to scale

Scaling guidance can be straightforward or complex. The most straightforward scaling guidance – simply based on, say, project budgets – is likely to be too blunt an instrument. Overly complex guidance tends to fall into disuse. A variety of increasingly complex alternatives are presented below.

7.4.1 Project characteristics

There are, in essence, five aspects of a project:

- cost
- time
- scope
- quality
- risk.

These five project dimensions are a modest extension of the oft quoted 'on time and on budget' or 'on time, on spec and on budget' mantras used by Project Managers.

The most straightforward way to categorise projects is to assess one or more of the above dimensions during Controlled Start. Sites may define two or three bands for each dimension and may also allocate a weighting to each band. These weightings can be summed up to create an overall complexity score for the project. Based on this score, elements of PRINCE2 should be implemented more formally. Alternatively, specific elements of PRINCE2 can be mandated if they score highly, for example more planning rigour if the project is complex.

7.4.1.1 Cost

Cost (resources) is the simplest and most comprehensive measure of project size. It is also fairly straightforward to state a monetary value. However, care must be taken to include possible hidden costs such as internal staff time; travel costs; hardware, software or equipment. This is particularly relevant in a non-commercial environment. Project costing can evolve into a very complex topic when charges for accommodation and central services are factored in.

Costing rules for projects should align with organisational financial procedures and should be agreed with the relevant finance department.

7.4.1.2 Time

The duration of a project can indicate the potential size of the project. Simplistically, longer projects are more difficult to manage as they are likely to be larger. At the other end of the scale, there can also be difficulties with managing very short projects, as mentioned earlier. The most straightforward projects to manage can be those that are of medium size.

Furthermore, the pace of a project can be a scaling factor. There are various metrics relating project duration to typical project sizes. These have been gathered from both PRINCE2 and non-PRINCE2 environments and so have not been quoted in this book. Local cultures need to be factored into such project metrics. In essence, these metrics show that, for a given organisation, there is a natural upper limit to the fastest pace of a project of a given size. This is determined by mundane factors such as the rate at which a team can be assembled.

A refinement of assessing time and cost separately is to compare cost and time to identify the project pace. If the project is being undertaken at, or even beyond, the fastest normal pace, it will be more difficult to manage. This pace factor can be used as a sixth project characteristic.

7.4.1.3 Scope

The third factor to be considered is the complexity or breadth of a project. A project being undertaken for one organisational unit on one site is clearly more straightforward to manage than one covering many different organisational units or split across many sites. Similarly, projects involving a range of disciplines will be more difficult to manage.

This factor can also be amplified to cover not just the initial scope of a project but also a prediction of the level of change within the project. At first sight, it would seem to be impossible to predict the anticipated level of issues. Nevertheless, Project Boards must set some level of Change Budget within a project during initiation. One simple rule of thumb is that the larger the permissible Change Budget, the more effort that will be expended on assessing and implementing changes and consequently the greater the complexity of a project. Large Change Budgets would be prudent, for example, if a step change in capability is being introduced.

7.4.1.4 Quality

The next factor to be considered is the criticality of products. If products are safety-critical, business-critical or must be highly reliable, then testing will be considerably more rigorous. This will add an additional layer to project management.

7.4.1.5 Risk

Finally, the risk profile of a project should be considered. If the inherent or business risk profile of a project is high, additional effort must be expended to manage those risks. Also, if a project has to operate at a high level of risk, for whatever reason, the project management task will be more difficult because that risk has to be monitored carefully. On the other hand, if there is a need to maintain a very low-risk profile for a project, the project management effort will again increase because risks will have to be foreseen and countermeasures will be required to mitigate the risks.

7.4.2 A matrix

As is readily apparent from the preceding section, a simple checklist for, say, five characteristics can easily be expanded to cover several dozen topics. If a single figure for project complexity is calculated the tailoring that emerges will be very crude. A more refined technique is to link particular elements of PRINCE2 to particular project characteristics. So, for example, the frequency and formality of risk analysis could be linked to the level of risk within a project.

Several characteristics of a project may trigger the use of any individual element of PRINCE2. Therefore, this type of guidance tends to be presented as a matrix, showing project characteristics on one axis and PRINCE2 elements on a second axis. Though superficially attractive, there are a number of weaknesses associated with guidance matrices. Staff must be taught how to use a matrix at a time when they are probably also learning PRINCE2. Also, it is very difficult to test all possible permutations on a matrix. Therefore, the Project Management team must still assess what emerges from a guidance matrix and decide whether it is appropriate. This can be more complex than working from first principles. Finally, for projects of medium complexity, a matrix often recommends the use of everything in PRINCE2. If this is likely to be the case, the matrix becomes an unnecessary extra step to be considered during Controlled Start. On balance, matrices are often poorly understood and fall into disrepute.

7.4.3 A checklist

What appears to be the next level of complexity can actually be both effective and straight-forward to use. There are key criteria associated with each of the processes within Controlled Start. The key criteria from

- the six processes within Starting a Project (SU)
- the six processes within Initiating a Project (IP)
- Authorising Initiation (DP1) and Authorising a Project (DP2)

can be extracted from an electronic version of the PRINCE2 manual and promulgated as a checklist or questionnaire.

The Project Management team record against each key criterion either that it has been met (and cross-refers to the relevant portion of the Project Initiation Document) or the reason for not meeting the criterion.

The following example shows one key criterion from Designing the Project Management Team (SU2) and a possible response:

> 'Have all the roles and responsibilities been allocated? If not, are the exclusions justified?'

> *'The roles of Project Manager and Team Manager have been combined, because …'*

This exercise could be done verbally, possibly in the presence of Project Assurance, or it could be documented. This document can then be linked to the Lessons Learned Report and audited, either during or after the project's completion.

8

SCALING COMPONENTS

This chapter considers how individual PRINCE2 components can be reduced in complexity.

8.1 Organisation

8.1.1 Cross-reference to the PRINCE2 method

- Organisation component and roles and responsibilities

8.1.2 Example

An in-house consultancy uses PRINCE2 for short assignments (down to 20 person days) treating them as small projects. A senior consultant acts as Senior Supplier; the person requesting the assignment acts as the Executive and Senior User. There is no Project Assurance, and the consultant carrying out the assignment acts as Project Manager, Team Manager and the project team.

8.1.3 Scaling

Scaling the Project Management team is primarily about role and function consolidation. In a small project, one person can fulfil a number of roles. However, the roles of Project Board and Project Manager should not be combined as their amalgamation seriously weakens control and blurs the distinction between strategic and day-to-day control. The roles on the Project Board, however, may be combined.

Even on a small project there will be a Customer/Supplier environment, although probably a non-commercial one. Therefore, the roles of the Executive and Senior User could be first to be combined, however there may be conflict of interests. One way round this is for the Executive/Senior User to appoint two individuals to carry out Project Assurance: one looking after the user interests and the other the business interests. For a very small project, one person can carry out all three Project Board roles. Some refer to a one-person Project Board as a project sponsor, although that term is also frequently used to define someone from corporate or programme management who issues the initial remit for the project. 'Project sponsor' is not a PRINCE2 role. A project sponsor, however, can still appoint Project Assurance.

On smaller projects, the Project Manager will probably be much closer to the Project Board. The Board will then be in a better position to carry out their own Project Assurance rather than appointing another individual to fulfil this role. The role of Team Manager is optional as the Project Manager of a small project can carry out those responsibilities. At the same time, the Project Manager may also undertake the role of Project Support and, indeed, be a team member. The difficulty here for the Project Manager is that he or she must balance the effort of managing the project against the effort of doing the work. This can introduce additional risks.

Within larger projects, there is likely to be some distance between the Project Manager and the Project Board. This can be physical, in terms of geographical distance, or hierarchical. So it is less likely that combined roles will be successful. On a very large project, scaling could mean breaking the generic PRINCE2 roles into multiple functions. Several Senior Users could be appointed and their responsibilities, for ensuring that all the final products work together, clearly defined. However, if a Project Board grows to more than about seven people it is likely to become indecisive and pace could suffer. User or Supplier groups can maintain broad-ranging senior management involvement without enlarging the Project Board, though. Project Assurance roles can also be fulfilled by a number of individuals, as can Project Support; departments such as Internal Audit may be willing to undertake Project Assurance. Other roles such as Change Authority, Quality Review and Configuration Librarian can become full-time posts.

8.1.4 Implementing

Different organisational units can be reluctant to work together – the silo mentality. The perfect Project Manager should have an empathy with the business, user and supplier stakeholder interests. Often the Project Manager will be regarded as being partisan and representing only one single stakeholder group. The solution is to appoint effective Project Assurance from the other stakeholders. For example, if a Project Manager is perceived to be from the user community it might be appropriate to appoint business and supplier Project Assurance.

For larger projects, some organisations attempt to appoint several Project Managers. However, when the responsibilities of these individuals are examined, usually one of them can be appointed as overall Project Manager, with the others fulfilling Team Manager roles. The key is to identify the individual with day-to-day responsibility for co-ordination across the project.

8.2 Controls

8.2.1 Cross-reference to the PRINCE2 method

- Controls component and Product Description outlines for associated reports

8.2.2 Example

The armed forces are comfortable using face-to-face briefings, without taking minutes, when circumstances dictate. A military unit that developed software applications normally used conventional PRINCE2 controls. When required to produce new applications in a very short timescale, as a result of a national emergency, the unit continued to use PRINCE2. However, as all the staff involved were comfortable with undocumented face-to-face meetings the projects were controlled, very rigorously, but without written documentation during Controlled Progress.

8.2.3 Scaling

The Controls component is broken down into Controlled Start, Controlled Progress and Controlled Close. In general, each of these parts of the component consists of a series of events (meetings) and reports. They also involve some underlying concepts. By looking in detail at the concepts, one can understand how to scale this component without losing its value.

Controlled Start involves the concept of using Starting Up a Project (SU), Initiating a Project (IP), the first two processes from Directing a Project (DP1 and DP2) and Stage Selection. The underlying idea is that there are one or more initial interactions between the Project Manager and the Project Board, at which the control environment for the project is agreed. This is followed by the definition of all the other routine occasions on which the Project Manager and the Project Board will meet – the stage boundaries. Stated this way, Controlled Start can be scaled by reducing what appears to be a long series of separate processes, involving many documents, down to a smaller number of interactions amongst a group people, which are then suitably documented.

Controlled Progress is underpinned by the concept of Management by Exception. The plan, including Tolerance, is agreed between the Project Manager and the Project Board. If progress on the Stage is within Tolerance, only highlights are reported. If the stage exceeds, or is forecast to exceed, Tolerance, the nature of the Exception is reported. Once again, the concept can be implemented without recourse to long meetings and even longer documents. In essence, the statement 'Let me know how things are going generally, but if anything goes wrong send me an e-mail' is Controlled Progress.

Finally, Controlled Close is about ensuring that four aspects of project closure are being considered:

- products have been delivered
- products will be taken forward or supported after the project
- lessons have been learned
- benefit realisation will be checked.

Controlled Close can be done as a conversation between the Project Manager and Project Board, with simple documentation of all the outcomes.

8.2.4 Implementing

All organisations operate with sets of controls. These may be formal or informal but they are likely to be deeply rooted in the organisational culture. PRINCE2 does not impose new formats of control on an organisation. If a Project Manager makes informal notes of a meeting, this is still a form of Daily Log and can prove to be a useful record of events. If an organisation has informal meetings, then this is the type of meeting that should be used within a PRINCE2 project. If an organisation is comfortable with comprehensive documentation, then this approach should be adopted within a PRINCE2 project.

When tailoring PRINCE2 controls, the key is to follow the underlying concepts within the Controls component and to choose styles of meetings and reports that match organisational culture.

8.3 Plans

8.3.1 Cross-reference to the PRINCE2 method

- Plans component and Product Description outlines for plans

8.3.2 Example

A small company commissioned an equally small marketing firm to undertake several assignments. Overall, the work would take several months and involve about 20 person days of effort, so the customer regarded the work as a project.

The Project Manager, from the Customer organisation, sent an e-mail confirming which products were required and how they should be released for checking a few days before an agreed meeting at the end of the project. The e-mail noted that various User and marketing staff would undertake certain activities, and defined the circumstances in which the marketing company should come back to the Customer. The e-mail also confirmed the cost of the overall exercise. The owner of the marketing company replied, agreeing to the terms.

This e-mail contained all the necessary components of a PRINCE2 Plan. It also contained an appropriate amount of the detail from a Project or Stage Plan, as illustrated in the relevant Product Description outlines.

8.3.3 Scaling

Planning is carried out for a number of purposes including:

- clarification – verifying the target
- communication – sharing the goals with others
- commitment – gaining agreement to the objectives
- control – as the baseline against which to measure progress.

Any plan should be tested for its contribution to these aims. If the depth or rigour of a plan does not contribute to one or more of the above purposes, consideration should be given to making this aspect of the plan less formal.

Other aspects of the plan – for example money, deliverables, resources, risks, etc. – should not be omitted lightly. For a particularly important aspect, a graphical presentation may be a useful way of presenting the information. Often a graphical plan places an emphasis on the detail of what should happen if things 'go well'. However, the essence of a PRINCE2 plan is also to show what assumptions have been made and what actions will be taken when things 'go wrong', that is when the plan exceeds Tolerance. The PRINCE2 method does not say that a plan is a Gantt chart. A Gantt chart may form one element of a plan, if it is appropriate to include a graphical plan and if the start and end dates of activities are particularly significant. A 'to do' list is an equally valid low-level plan. Thus, if product delivery is important, a Product Checklist could be included.

Yet another way of looking at a plan is to consider it to be the contract between a Project Manager and a Project Board. It should only contain those elements that are considered to be essential by at least one of those parties.

8.3.4 Implementing

Culturally, organisations have become attached to Gantt charts. They are presented by Project Managers to Project Boards and are regarded by Project Boards as a sign that proper planning has been undertaken. However, many Project Managers do not understand how to construct a Gantt chart and fail to create an appropriate Product Checklist or dependency model. Consequently, when they try to use the scheduling algorithms within the software package that can also draw the Gantt chart, the plan collapses. All too often the solution for the Project Manager is to switch off the scheduling function within the software package and instead to constrain activities, etc. in order to present the picture that he or she wished to show. These Gantt charts may reflect neither resource over-commitment nor a realistic critical path. When challenged, the Project Manager is on uncertain ground. If the Project Board wishes the project to be completed more quickly, or at a lower budget, the Project Manager cannot alter or vary assumptions, constraints or estimates because he or she knows that the plan has a weak basis. Therefore, the Project Manager is forced to comply with unrealistic demands.

The construction of a soundly based Gantt chart is covered in more detail in later sections on product-based planning. Suffice to say, submission of a Gantt chart that is not backed up by an appropriate level of automatic calculation of critical paths is a false economy.

Furthermore, a plan is not a narrative history of a project. It is a statement of the intended actions to be taken in the future. Culturally, organisations that are risk-averse are comfortable with including a narrative because it allows individuals to avoid or not accept responsibility. However, within a project, a plan that includes significant amounts of unnecessary narrative blurs the definition of roles, slows the pace of plan creation and makes it easier to omit essential elements from them.

Overall, cultural influences may have a detrimental effect on the creation of light but effective Project or Stage Plans. Levels of Plan allow each plan to be comprehensive, sufficiently accurate and short.

8.4 Stages

8.4.1 Cross-reference to the PRINCE2 method

- Stages or Control components

8.4.2 Example

The first stage in any project is an Initiation Stage. This can be equated with the Controlled Start of a project. The remainder of the work of many projects – that is, simple projects lasting for only a few months – can be completed within a single stage. Therefore a large proportion of projects are merely two-stage projects.

8.4.3 Scaling

This can be demonstrated by a brief analysis of stage metrics. The PRINCE2 method does not state exactly how long a stage should be. A useful rule of thumb, however, is that a stage should last 1–10 elapsed weeks. Stages should be shorter when there is greater risk, uncertainty or complexity, for example at the beginning and end of projects. Stages can be longer when risk is low, typically in the middle of projects.

When it comes to tailoring PRINCE2, the concept of the two-stage project is a powerful one. There may be difficulties conveying the concepts of Management and Technical Stages. Project Board members are likely to have had bad experiences of being inundated with technical detail. Meanwhile, specialists will be reluctant to think of anything other than Technical Stages. This problem evaporates in the two-stage project.

Levels of Plan also become irrelevant in the two-stage project. When a project is sufficiently small, the Project Plan is the Stage Plan, and there is no need to create formal Team Plans. Should the project go into Exception, however, there will be a need to assess which products have been completed and to create a new Stage Plan. Finally, in a two-stage project, Managing Stage Boundaries (SB) and End of Assessments are not required. When implementing the PRINCE2 method there is an argument for first applying PRINCE2 on two-stage projects, before using the method in more complex projects. While experience will build more slowly, success is likely to be greater.

8.4.4 Implementing

Implementing the concept of stages within a culture is often a matter of judging the power gradient between levels within the hierarchy. The power gradient is flat if there is little regard within the organisational structure. The caricature of a dot.com company – where all the staff are young, casually dressed and recruited yesterday – is a good, if slightly extreme, example of a flat power gradient. The opposite extreme is the caricature (perhaps unfair) of the hospital consultant, who is in charge of everything but is only prepared to be involved in medical matters. Where the power gradient is flat, Project Boards will wish to be much more closely involved in projects and to define shorter stages. On the other hand, where there is a steep gradient, senior management will be much less keen to be involved in the day-to-day workings of a project. They will consequently delegate more to the Project Manager and will prefer stage lengths to be increased.

The Project Manager may have to assess the costs associated with additional Stage Boundaries or the risks of insufficient Stage Boundaries.

8.5 Risk

8.5.1 Cross-reference to the PRINCE2 method

- Risk component and associated Product Description outlines

8.5.2 Example

An extract from a real Risk Log reads:

> Risk – the project may overrun.
>
> Countermeasure – all efforts will be made to prevent any overrun.

This is an example of a generalised approach to risks. The risk itself is far too vague to be manageable: it would be more useful to identify the causes of the potential overrun. In this project, the underlying cause was too many sub-critical paths, each with a very low float and all of which were closely interdependent.

Furthermore, the risk line states the event, rather than stating the adverse consequences of the event. The event is that the project may overrun; the adverse consequences could, for example, be delayed realisation of benefits, missing a deadline or increased costs.

The countermeasure line uses the passive voice: 'The mat was sat upon'; as opposed to the active voice: 'The cat sat on the mat'. This allows the risk owner to be omitted. A more suitable Risk Log entry would be:

> Risk – The project may overrun because there is insufficient float in the dependency network. The consequence of this would be delayed realisation of benefits.
>
> Countermeasure – The Project Manager will identify and break a significant number of dependencies when producing the next Stage Plan.

8.5.3 Scaling

Practitioners need to consider the concepts underlying the Risk component in order to apply it effectively. The PRINCE2 terminology is particularly precise in this area: dealing with risk involves risk analysis and risk management.

Risk analysis is no more than identifying and thinking about how to manage the adverse consequences of future events. This means deciding on the particular actions to be taken when dealing with specific risks. This will inevitably occur some time before the risk may occur.

Even in the smallest project it is useful to document risks in some formal Risk Log. Once risks have been recorded in a log then managing them is much more an attitude of mind than a particular set of processes. The key is specific activities must be inserted into plans to deal with risks.

Risk management is the incorporation of specific, costed, resourced actions into plans to have some effect on potential risks, and ensuring that defined actions are followed through. Once an activity has been placed within a plan it should be treated in exactly the same way as any other activity in the plan. In other words, it must be resourced, there must be some formal checking at the end of the activity to ensure that the outcome is as expected, and the risk product – just like any other product – must be controlled.

Scaling the management of risk can, therefore, be as simple as carrying out regular risk analysis and incorporating risk management into planning and control.

8.5.4 Implementing

The implementation of the management of risk depends on the underlying business culture surrounding the concept of risk. Many organisations are still more concerned with management of the status quo than the management of change. Such organisations are inherently risk-averse. The project champion will appreciate that risks can best be mitigated if they are clearly identified and described. However, in many cultures there is a subconscious view that discussion of risks will somehow raise the risk profile. These are cultures where the discussion of risk is discouraged. This is another area where the Project Manager is forced to weigh up the risk of not considering risks against the adverse reaction of the Project Management team if the management of risk is raised.

The next implementation issue concerns acceptance of responsibility. The pitfalls of generalised risk management are illustrated in the example above.

A further consideration when implementing the management of risk concerns commercial sensitivities. Often one partner to a contract maintains a confidential Risk Log that is not disclosed to the other partner. The PRINCE2 concept of two classes of Business Case – the Customer Business Case and the Supplier Business Case – is used as a justification for the existence of 'shadow' documents. The consequences of this are discussed in Section 3.1.6, *The commercial environment.*

8.6 Quality

8.6.1 Cross-reference to the PRINCE2 method

- Quality component and Product Description outlines for associated management and quality products

8.6.2 Example

An experienced Project Manager joined an organisation that used PRINCE2. She was unfamiliar with the method and was reluctant to undergo lengthy training, given her considerable experience. A Project Assurance adviser persuaded her to adopt a quality-centred approach by arranging for her to produce Product Checklists that were also used as Quality Logs. Introduction of just this combined document proved to be sufficient to maintain the required quality-centred approach.

8.6.3 Scaling

Quality is a concept that was a popular management theme in the 1980s. Having subsequently disappeared from view, it is now reappearing. Quality-centred approaches to projects encourage staff to build in quality at the beginning of the work. This is the concept that underlies the Quality component within PRINCE2. It is a very straightforward and powerful concept. Quality Expectations are established and then amplified before planning has started. Plans are expressed in terms of the checks that products must pass. Progress is then judged on the basis of products being fit for purpose rather than effort having been expended.

This approach is followed throughout the project: from the initial establishment of Quality Expectations with the Project Board; through defining Work Packages, based on the required quality in products; to reporting progress to the Project Board. These ideas are inherent in the sequence of planning. If Quality Expectations are stated before a plan is created, it is much more likely that the plan will be built to deliver those Quality Expectations. Similarly, if progress is reported based on the fitness for purpose of products, then quality checking will perforce have to have been carried out.

The ideas underlying the Quality component can be implemented within a project by the use of one, simple management product – the Product Checklist.

The Product Checklist is created during Planning. To the casual reader of the PRINCE2 method it then seems to disappear. In fact, it becomes part of the Stage Plan and then the Work Package. When it is next seen it has been expanded to include the results of quality checks and is referred to as the Quality Log. This is circulated with the Checkpoint Report and summarised to the Project Board in the Highlight Report. Highlight Reports ultimately lead to the End Stage Report. If champions insist on using a Product Checklist or Quality Log this will take them a long way down the road of implementing the PRINCE2 concept of quality.

8.6.4 Implementing

Implementing a quality-centred approach to planning often comes up against different definitions of the word 'quality'. For example, some cultures interpret the word to mean 'excellence'. Some would claim a Rolls-Royce is a quality car, meaning it is expensive. When managers from such organisations hear a discussion about quality, they assume that the Project Manager wishes to 'gold-plate' products. A more prosaic definition of quality is 'fitness for purpose'. Using this definition, one could argue that a Rolls-Royce would be inappropriate for inner-city commuting.

The underlying issues surrounding implementation are communication and expectations needing to be set, at the latest during Planning Quality in IP1.

A similar problem occurs when Customer and Supplier organisations, whether linked by commercial or non-commercial arrangements, have differing concepts of quality testing. For example, an IT department may have preferred methods of testing involving regression tests, test scripts and other jargon. A user community may not recognise that this testing is being done on their behalf, in order to demonstrate that products meet the users' quality expectations. This breakdown in communication can cause resentment among stakeholder groups at having to participate in externally imposed quality checks. The solution is to build a consensus on how quality will be tested. This is the Quality Plan. Fortunately, as with many of the suggestions for a scaled-down PRINCE2 method, it does not have to be a long or even a formal document. The key is that the right people are involved in the discussion.

8.7 Change Control

8.7.1 Cross-reference to the PRINCE2 method

- Change Control component and Product Description outlines for associated management products

8.7.2 Example

Nearly 100 years ago the Hawthorne Light and Power Company manufactured electric light bulbs. The quality of bulbs was so poor that the owners called in early management consultants. The general view was that the light levels in the factory were too low. The consultants therefore increased the factory's illumination and, as predicted, quality went up. Lighting was expensive then so the consultants next decided to reduce the lighting to find out what level of illumination had to be provided to achieve the required level of quality. The consultants were surprised when the light level settled below that which had been in place when they were called in, for the quality of the finished light bulbs remained high. After some further experimentation one of the consultants realised that the improvement in quality was caused by the interest that the consultants had taken in the workers, not by the level of factory illumination.

There is a parallel between this example and projects. Whenever a project is started in a particular user area the workers in that area may be asked about how working practices can be improved. As the project progresses they may continue to be consulted and be shown proto-types of new working practices. It is hardly surprising that in such a scenario workers might think about how they could do their work differently. Additional new ideas will tend to emerge, as the project progresses. These new ideas are called Requests for Change. These are an inevitable side effect of involving people in how they might do their work in different ways. Therefore, virtually all projects will have to include a mechanism for capturing and assessing changes.

8.7.3 Scaling

The concept behind Change Control is that almost every project will trigger a desire for changes in the User community. Allowance should also be made for mandatory external changes, for example central government imposing new procedures on local government. The only projects where there would be no Change Control would be those where no change proposals could be tolerated. These are very rare, however an example of just such an instance is the millennium bug. Just before the millennium there were a small number of Y2K pre-paration projects that were started very late and ran for only a few months or even weeks. Some of these projects were under such an immovable time deadline that no changes at all could be envisaged. Such projects needed no Change Control mechanism. All other projects will require some Change Control mechanism albeit, in many cases, a straightforward one. For small projects, it is perfectly acceptable for the Change Control mechanism to be created only once changes start to emerge.

8.7.4 Implementing

The level of change, and therefore the amount of change control, can be seen to be a result of various factors:

- length of time since working practices were last reviewed
- size of the project
- amount of involvement and consultation built into the project culture
- precision of any requirement's specification
- familiarity with the business area and solution
- stability of the decision-making process and culture
- political background.

Some of these factors have more to do with the underlying organisation than with the isolated shape of the project. These cultural factors must be considered when scaling PRINCE2.

Narrowly, a straightforward Change Control procedure need be little more than a brief log of Requested Changes and some modest Configuration Management. More broadly, the PRINCE2 champion should provoke a debate on the expected level of change. This should be based as much on cultural factors as on the size of the project. Once the level of expected change has been agreed, a suitable Change Control mechanism can be put into place.

8.8 Configuration Management

8.8.1 Cross-reference to the PRINCE2 method

- Configuration Management component and Product Description outlines for associated management products

8.8.2 Example

An international dot.com incubator set up an IT company to develop Internet applications for the dot.com businesses that were being created. What the new venture lacked in experience they made up for in enthusiasm. They were admirably energetic and focused in their work.

Their approach to Configuration Management was no less vigorous. They developed document-based management product templates, each of which contained a detailed document audit trail. As a result, some single-page documents, for example simple Product Descriptions, could actually be three pages long once the two pages of Configuration Management information were appended. Such standards did feel a little onerous on short projects, and it was difficult to explain to staff that the burden was a cultural rather than PRINCE2-inherited one.

This example relates particularly to version control, but similar responses do occur when complex Configuration Management methods are imposed within a project.

8.8.3 Scaling

Components tend to be self-explanatory. 'Stages', for example, are recognised by most managers once the underlying idea is explained. Scaling Configuration Management presents a particular problem. Configuration Management tends to be seen as a specialist activity and consequently one that may not be of interest to the Project Board.

The first issue to address is communicating the ideas behind Configuration Management to the Project Board. These should not be trivialised nor come across as overly specialist. The need for Configuration Management should be dictated by an assessment of factors such as:

- the importance of products
- geographical dispersal
- access restrictions, such as confidentiality and security
- the likelihood and impact of loss or damage
- the complexity of inter-relationships.

The likely scale of the vulnerability of each product should then be assessed before it is nominated as a Configuration Item. Then the best way of controlling this Configuration Item should be decided. There are two sides to Configuration Management: the management of document-based Configuration Items, which may be management or specialist products, and the management of specialist Configuration Items.

Often Configuration Management standards are based more on past experience rather than the needs within the project. Some sites implement overly rigorous document-control standards and fail to consider how specialist products will be controlled. There is a particular weakness when linking products of different types. For example, in a call centre project, common Configuration Management should be applied to business procedures, staff knowledge (achieved through training) and IT support systems. In project management terms, Configuration Management should be considered as a cross-functional discipline, not as a technical ghetto.

8.8.4 Implementing

There is a tendency to over-manage document-based Configuration Items. Frequently, projects will attempt to apply overly rigorous Configuration Management to the initial management products and, as a result, the project team regards project management as being overly bureaucratic. The net result is that the well-meaning Configuration Management standards quickly fall by the wayside. **It is better to introduce less rigorous standards that are maintained throughout the project.**

Configuration Management standards for management products can be less rigorous than those applied to document-based specialist products. Management products need only be controlled for the life of the project, as any project comprises a temporary management environment which will be discarded once the project is finished. The situation may be slightly different when there are strongly enforced cross-project standards (covered in Section 4.1.3.1).

Regarding specialist Configuration Management: the IT industry has made great strides in recent decades in improving Configuration Management from a low base. Other industries, notably engineering, have traditionally maintained higher standards of Configuration Management. Therefore, **the Project Manager should think carefully about the target audience when discussing specialist Configuration Management.** Staff with existing high standards of Configuration Management will not take kindly to a newcomer talking enthusiastically about standards that are in fact lower than the site standards. The key is to know your audience.

89

8.9 Business Case

8.9.1 Cross-reference to the PRINCE2 method

- Business Case component and associated management products

8.9.2 Example

A small company decided to introduce new IT hardware and software. They used a supplier to install the system and train the staff to use it as an aid to producing an illustrated parts catalogue. The owner stated that this catalogue would enable staff to identify parts described to them over the phone. It would also mean that they could provide better customer service. It would save staff time, and portions of the catalogue could be used as marketing material. Considering cost, the managing director stated that he felt the system was worth having. This was the Business Case for the Project.

8.9.3 Scaling

As with the scaling of other PRINCE2 components, an understanding of the concept underlying the Business Case will assist greatly in scaling this element. A Business Case is the basis for justifying the project and a tool for deciding to continue with or close a project. It should, therefore, contain just enough information to enable the Project Board to decide if the project is justified and to make sensible major decisions.

There must be a set of identified benefits that can be attributed to the introduction of a product – the final product of the project. Those benefits must be solely attributable to that product, not to other initiatives in the customer organisation. On completion of the project, it must be possible to track those benefits in order to confirm that the project was worth doing.

The treatment of the Business Case within the PRINCE2 method can be perceived to be light. This is deliberate because Business Cases must be firmly based in the culture of the customer organisation. It would be inappropriate for the PRINCE2 method to be prescriptive about the content of a Business Case.

Once a Business Case exists it must be maintained during the life of the project, notably at Stage Boundaries, so that a comparison can be made between the original Business Case and the situation at the end of the project (in the End Project Report). Given the existence of a Business Case, it can be used as a control tool by the Project Manager.

A more sophisticated technique is to apportion benefits between intermediate products. This does not need to be done to a high degree of precision. Even an arbitrary split of benefits between products is a statement by the project management team on the relative importance of different aspects of the project. Although only approximate, it can be more useful, than not, to carry out benefits apportionment. The simplest method of apportioning benefits is to divide them roughly equally among products at the same level on a Product Breakdown Structure. This technique can be considered to be a basic form of earned value analysis, which relies on products at the same level on a Product Breakdown Structure being of broadly comparable worth. When each product is then broken down to a lower level, the benefits are once again split. If the higher-level product is an integration product, some of the benefits will remain at the higher level with the rest split among the lower-level products. If the higher-level product is a collective product, no benefits are retained at the higher level; they are all taken down to the lower level.

(The terms 'integration product' and 'collective products' may be new to some readers. The 2002 edition of the PRINCE2 manual has introduced these concepts in the Product Breakdown Structure technique. An integration product is an intermediate product with a meaningful test of the inter-operability of several lower-level products. A wheel is an integration product if it is necessary to test that the tyre fits the rim. A collective product simply groups some lower-level products – the cutlery consists of the knives and the forks.)

8.9.4 Implementing

The nature of benefits is covered in more detail in *Managing Successful Programmes* (TSO (The Stationery Office), 1999, ISBN 0 11 330016 6). However, the key to appreciating benefits in a particular culture is to understand clearly what the organisation values are. Often a benefit is no more than whatever a senior manager judges to be of worth. If the manager has budget authority in a particular area he or she may be empowered to state that something is worth a particular amount. That may be a valid Business Case. This idea is at the root of intangible benefits.

In more commercial organisations there may be clearly defined rules on how to define a Business Case, and these should be complied with when implementing PRINCE2. In government, the situation is more difficult. There is a growing tendency for departments to have service plans, which state the worth of the various services offered to the community. The concept has been applied in areas as diverse as the value of a particular weapons system to the relative importance of different types of social service. Where sound service plans exist, they provide a very useful starting point for creating a Business Case.

9
SCALING PROCESSES

This chapter looks at how each individual process can be reduced in complexity.

9.1 Starting up a Project

9.1.1 Cross-reference to the PRINCE2 method

- Starting Up a Project (SU) process and associated management products, notably the Project Mandate, Project Brief, Project Approach, Job Descriptions and Risk Log

9.1.2 Scaling

Sufficient Start Up must be completed for a Project Board to confirm the fundamental principle of Authorising Initiation (DP1) – 'Is the project sensible?' Just enough effort should be expended to allow this question to be answered. Documents should be comprehensive enough to allow the basis of this decision to be baselined, no more. Many sites condense Starting Up a Project into completion of a single multi-purpose form.

Most of the documentation produced at the end of Starting Up a Project need only be valid for a matter of days, until Initiating the Project is completed. By then, all the products of Start Up will have been subsumed into the products of Initiation. The exception is the Project Mandate. Formally an input to Starting Up a Project, the Project Mandate is likely to be refined within the process. It will continue to be referred to throughout the life of the project as the trigger for it. However, it can be a very informal product and may not be in a format that allows it to be referred to easily. It may be more appropriate, therefore, to regard the Project Brief as the product that describes the initial vision for the project.

There are five significant management products produced within Starting Up a Project:

- the Project Brief
- the Project Approach
- the Risk Log
- the Organisation Structure
- Job Descriptions.

The Project Brief is an amplification of the Project Mandate and ultimately is expanded into the Project Initiation Document. As an evolving product, its role is to allow the Project Board to judge the value of committing resources to Initiating the Project. For smaller projects this decision will be more straightforward because the resources required for Initiation will be lower. The resources needed for the initiation of a smaller project will, of course, be a larger proportion of the total project management effort than would be the case on a larger project. Therefore, the information required in a Project Brief will be less, bringing the Project Brief closer in detail to a Project Mandate. These two documents can easily be combined into one.

The Project Approach is particularly important in projects with a commercial Customer/Supplier environment as it helps to identify the type of commercial partner. When there is a non-commercial Customer/Supplier environment the Project Approach may be less detailed. The Project Approach may not be put aside entirely, as it will include something about how the project is to be conducted. It can, however, be combined into a composite Project Mandate and Project Brief.

At this point in a project only a few major risks will be identified. Rather than recording them in a separate Risk Log they can be documented in the Project Brief.

The Organisation Structure for a simple project will contain fewer than the seven standard project roles: Executive, Senior Supplier, Senior User, Project Manager, Project Assurance, Project Support and Team Manager. Once again, a simpler structure can be documented within the Project Brief.

Job Descriptions can be stated explicitly or, more simply, reference can be made to the template Job Descriptions in the PRINCE2 manual. There is, however, a risk when referring to template Job Descriptions: there may be insufficient 'buy in' by the holders of the various posts. Even in a small project there is value in reviewing the Job Descriptions, as much to reinforce acceptance of the individual responsibilities as to tailor the descriptions to the precise circumstances of the project. When roles are combined there will inevitably be more changes to be made to the outline Job Descriptions.

In a very small project, Starting Up a Project and Initiating a Project may be combined even further, simplifying Controlled Start.

9.1.3 Implementing

Starting Up a Project sits outside the formal project environment. It may, therefore, form part of a local process. Many different organisations have procedures for starting projects. Starting Up a Project should be merged with these processes to avoid duplication. So, for example, if internal budgeting requires a particular form to be raised, prior to commencing a project, creation of this form should become part of Starting Up a Project and elements within Starting Up a Project that are covered by the local form should be omitted.

9.2 Initiating a Project

9.2.1 Cross-reference to the PRINCE2 method

- Initiating a Project (IP) process and associated management products, notably the Project Initiation Document

9.2.2 Scaling

It is mostly in the Initiating a Project process that all the many topics covered in this book should be considered. By the end of Initiating a Project there must be clarity about what the project is intended to achieve and how it will be managed. When Authorising a Project (DP2), the Project Board must confirm both the alignment of the project with wider business goals and a definition of an adequate project management environment. A snapshot of this information (a baseline) should also be kept.

Project Managers often say in jest that they will finish the Project Initiation Document before the end of the project … next time! This suggests that the purpose of the Project Initiation Document is misunderstood. The Project Initiation Document contains sufficient information to allow the Project Board to give approval for the commencement of the project and for the Project Manager to start working on it. If some interim document is published – with the intention of producing a more comprehensive Project Initiation Document in due course – and all are happy to use this as the basis of the project, the question must be posed as to why a more comprehensive document is required. On reflection, it may be unnecessary. The Project Initiation Document need not be a detailed exposition of what will happen within the project, should everything go according to plan. There is no need to include many tens of pages of Gantt charts: Project Initiation Documents can be as small as two pages of A4 text. The Project Initiation Document should instead be an exposition of what could or should be done if (some might say, when) the project deviates.

It can be useful to publish the Project Initiation Document in sections. The first section is the contract between the Project Manager and Project Board, which should only contain those elements that are considered essential by at least one or other party. This can be a very brief document with clear relevance to the parties. The second section can contain more mundane information on project procedures, for example how to log an Issue. These procedures must be published somewhere and the Project Initiation Document is the most appropriate location. This approach to the production of a Project Initiation Document usually results in a significantly smaller document.

Initiating a Project is also the phase when the policy is set for most of the components. The Organisation component will have already been considered during Starting Up a Project, but the Business Case should be considered. The different elements of PRINCE2 reinforce one another. Therefore, a project management environment based on the scaled implementation of multiple components will be both more robust and flexible than a project environment that focuses on only one or two of them. **The essence of Initiating a Project is to consider how the components will be applied in the project. This information then forms the content of the Project Initiation Document.**

9.2.3 Implementing

Many line organisations produce templates for Project Initiation Documents. These tend to encourage Project Managers to put text under every heading, whether relevant or not. Regrettably, there is also a tendency for text to be copied from one Project Initiation Document to another. A narrative history of the project to date may be included, which is not a PRINCE2 requirement. This latter tendency seems to have emerged because staff wish to put the project into a wider context. Sometimes there can also be an element of avoiding responsibility for a project, or claiming credit. Though understandable, given the politics within line organisations, these tendencies do not contribute to effective project management. The net effect is that Project Initiation Documents become larger and larger.

It is better if each Project Initiation Document is distinctly different, sometimes having sections removed or added as appropriate. This also presents an opportunity to consider which aspects of project management have traditionally been used, if any should be dropped and if others should be adopted. However, if a more flexible approach is taken to the contents of Project Initiation Documents, there is then a balance to be struck between the comfort zone of the team and moving PRINCE2 forward.

9.3 Planning

9.3.1 Cross-reference to the PRINCE2 method

- Planning (PL) process and associated management products, notably Project and Stage Plans

9.3.2 Example

Plans for small to medium-sized projects can be presented as an A4 Gantt chart or a Product Checklist with a few covering notes.

9.3.3 Scaling

The Planning process is intended to be a repeatable method for generating a sufficiently comprehensive plan. The scalability section within the *Planning* chapter of the PRINCE2 manual does go a long way towards making this clear. What does not emerge quite so clearly, however, is the broad group of people involved in Planning. A Project Plan should involve members of the Project Board (or, on a larger project, their representatives) and the Project Manager. For a Stage Plan, the Project and Team Managers should participate. Each of these groups should work with one another on the creation of their respective plan(s).

Formally, each of the sub-processes within Planning can become individual agenda items for a planning workshop. More informally, they can be individual points that are considered by a planning group as they construct a plan. This set of work steps has two less familiar characteristics: being product-based and quality-led. Product Descriptions encapsulate both characteristics.

Product-based planning can be put into context when tailoring the Planning process. Product-based planning is an adjunct to the Planning process, specifically within Defining and Analysing Products (PL2). It is not an alternative to the more familiar approach of activity-based planning, merely an addition. For example, it assists practitioners in understanding the scope of the project, intangible products, quality requirements and dependencies. Nevertheless, product-based planning is completed by the end of Identifying Activities and Dependencies (PL3). The remainder of Planning is activity-based.

The other characteristic within Planning is a quality-led approach. How products are to be checked comes at an early point within Planning, before activities are identified. Subsequently, the checking of products is used as an input to Controlling a Stage.

The output of the Planning process should be no more than a plan containing sufficient detail for all concerned, without the inclusion of spurious detail. This goal is reinforced by the concept of Levels of Plan within PRINCE2. Further detail is recorded in the plan at the next lower level and is generated later in the project, nearer the time at which products will be completed. If an organisation is unfamiliar with planning, Levels of Plan can introduce them gently to the concept. If the essence of a plan can be clearly communicated on a simple Gantt chart then this is a very appropriate format. PRINCE2 proposes an alternative, the Product Checklist, which puts rather more emphasis on the Products and slightly less emphasis on timescales. There is additional detail on the format of plans in Section 8.3.

9.3.4 Implementing

Most of this book concerns scaling PRINCE2 down for smaller projects. In implementing Planning, the difficulty is as likely to come from scaling up the method for larger projects. In such an environment there is likely to be widespread use of deterministic scheduling tools. In other words, there may be an attempt to define an environment where all staff work is recorded in advance. As organisations grow they often make greater and greater efforts to ensure more precision in predicting work.

PRINCE2 takes an alternative approach. Decision-making is delegated to a lower level, where appropriate. This is known as Management by Exception. If a Project Manager or Team Manager can take decisions within their competence, they have the authority to do so. The manager responsible for executing a plan has some freedom to vary it without referring this information to higher authority.

Management by Exception and a centrally collated repository of plans (as discussed in Section 4.3, *Tools*) can come into direct conflict. If PRINCE2 is to be operated in an environment with a rigidly controlled repository of plans, Project and Stage Tolerances must be reduced significantly.

9.4 Directing a Project

9.4.1 Cross-reference to the PRINCE2 method

- Directing a Project (DP) process and associated management products, notably Ad Hoc Guidance and Authorisations to Proceed

9.4.2 Example

When implementing a new management information system and associated procedures the senior management team of a medium-sized organisation appointed one of their number as Project Manager. Although the project was planned to last for more than a year, they signalled that they did not wish to break the project into stages. Despite using some parts of PRINCE2 during the day-to-day running of the project, it dragged on for more than twice as long as planned and still failed to deliver the expected culture change. It proved awkward to convince the senior management team that the difficulties with the project stemmed from their interpretation of Directing a Project rather than from a problem within the project itself.

In contrast, the senior managers of a small and vibrant software development company held weekly meetings to review the status of each project. Although they were reluctant to admit it, these were effectively Stage Boundaries. The team argued that events were so fast-moving that they had to keep close control of projects. They were surprised that their Project Managers felt disenfranchised.

9.4.3 Scaling

Directing a Project as a series of formal Project Board meetings will be a familiar idea. The PRINCE2 method does not dictate the level of formality within Directing a Project. The scalability section within the Directing a Project portion of the PRINCE2 manual emphasizes that reports may be received orally. Sensibly, the method points out that decisions should be documented so that they can be referred to at a later date. Tailoring Directing a Project often comes down to identifying a culturally suitable format that strikes the right balance between over- and under-involvement by a Project Board.

The underlying principle is that the Project Board should delegate day-to-day control of the project to the Project Manager. The Board, however, must exercise overall control and take key decisions. All concerned must understand the split between these responsibilities.

9.4.4 Implementing

When implementing Directing a Project, the Project Manager will not only be fully exposed to the line culture of one or more organisations but will also be dealing with senior managers. Understandably, these may be people who are more senior and more deeply indoctrinated in and wedded to the underlying culture. The PRINCE2 champion must sensitively set up Project Board meetings that are in tune with the culture and which can achieve the aims of Directing a Project. Put simply, the key is not to compete with the underlying culture of an organisation, unless the culture itself will hinder project success. Instead, those implementing PRINCE2 should describe Directing a Project in terms that will have the necessary effect, rather than in terms of a particular format. So, if a culture is wedded to the idea of formally documented meetings, the documentation of decisions need not be emphasized. In a very informal culture, documentation might have to be given a much higher profile. Where diaries become filled with meetings months in advance, the Project Manager may have to work hard to schedule Project Board meetings at times in the project that are meaningful (that is, event-based), as opposed to merely on a regular basis. In contrast, in a very informal organisation the pressure may be not to schedule meetings at all.

There may also be difficulties over terminology. For example, 'stages' may already have a particular meaning in the organisation that is at variance with the PRINCE2 usage of the word.

Project Managers, or PRINCE2 advocates on the Project Board, must keep in mind the fundamental principles of Directing a Project when adjusting their responses to the background culture. Those principles are Management by Exception and a balance of responsibilities across the Project Management team.

9.5 Managing Product Delivery

9.5.1 Cross-reference to the PRINCE2 method

- Managing Product Delivery (MP) process and associated management products, notably Work Packages, Quality Logs and Checkpoint Reports

9.5.2 Example

A manufacturer of servers and operating systems has adopted PRINCE2. In the marketplace, the company offers project management services, therefore positioning its staff as Project Managers. Many hundreds of their staff have been through PRINCE2 accreditation. The supply of IT infrastructure normally sits within a wider business project. Therefore, although this work may cost many tens of thousands of pounds, dollars or euros, the work of this company is, in PRINCE2 terms, providing a Work Package. Consequently, these 'Project Managers' are fulfilling the PRINCE2 role of Team Manager. The comprehensive documentation provided by the company maps onto PRINCE2 Work Packages.

In contrast, a small consultancy company that uses associates could define Work Packages in a simple free-format e-mail.

9.5.3 Scaling

Managing Product Delivery is detached from Controlling a Stage in order to provide a separation between a Customer-side Project Manager and commercial Suppliers. It also provides a separation between the Project Manager – who should be able to take a broad-ranging, management view of the project; and Team Managers – who may have a more restricted technical outlook.

A Work Package can be equated to the various types of contractual document that must inevitably exist. Excluding this contractual documentation, which is outside the scope of this book, the Work Package is no more than a statement of the work to be done, couched in terms of the tests that are to be performed on the products at the completion of the work. In addition, the Work Package will contain the practicalities for completing the work. These practicalities would not be in the Product Descriptions that are also contained within the Work Package. Where the contractual relationship permits, the Work Package can therefore be reduced to a straightforward composite document. Where there is one team on the project, the Work Package can even be a verbal agreement between the Project Manager and members of the project team.

Reporting from Managing Product Delivery should be subjective and objective: objective reports are made by completing a Quality Log; subjective information is included in the

Checkpoint Report. The Quality Log can be an extension of a Product Checklist. Where the team is co-located, this can be achieved by placing the Product Checklist on a visible notice board. Team members can then annotate completion of Work Packages by hand on the Product Checklist. A Team Manager can then give a Checkpoint Report verbally to the Project Manager by making a subjective assessment of the status of work, with reference to the Product Checklist.

Where one individual is performing the roles of both Project Manager and Team Manager, Managing Product Delivery can be simplified even further. In these circumstances, the 'CS/MP split' can be omitted. The three Managing Product Delivery processes and the closely associated processes within Controlling a Stage (CS) – of Authorising Work Packages (CS1), Assessing Progress (CS2) and Receiving Completed Work Packages (CS9) – can be merged. The key is to maintain objective reporting of product status.

Work Package closure can be simplified to a comparable level of formality. So, for example, if a Work Package is a simple, jointly drafted document, Work Package closure could be joint initialling of the document on completion of the work.

9.5.4 Implementing

Implementing Managing Product Delivery is dependent on geography and the Customer/Supplier environment. If teams are not co-located, or if there are contractual relationships, the process should be implemented more rigorously.

There may also be a cultural aspect to Managing Product Delivery where the subcontractor carrying out a Work Package has well-defined documentation procedures. It is often appropriate to adopt these standards by comparing them with the composition of a Work Package, only making additions where necessary. Similarly, standard reports can be compared to the content of a Checkpoint Report and Quality Log. In this area, changes often have to be made to ensure that products passing Quality Review are clearly logged.

9.6 Controlling a Stage

9.6.1 Cross-reference to the PRINCE2 method

- Controlling a Stage (CS) process and associated management products, notably End Stage Reports

9.6.2 Example

As an extremely large insurance project moved to its climax the intensity of Controlling a Stage increased. Much remedial evening work was being done so there was, in effect, a two-shift system in place. Checkpoint Reporting happened two, then three, times each day. This was done verbally beside a white board. As the weeks passed the Project Management team recognised the significance of these meetings and members of the Project Board began to attend them so that issues could be escalated and resolved during the course of the meeting.

9.6.3 Scaling

At first sight, Controlling a Stage can seem to be bewilderingly complex. This is under-standable, given that most Project Managers will spend perhaps 80% of their effort on Controlling a Stage.

In essence, the Project Manager is undertaking three tasks within Controlling a Stage:

- **ensuring scheduled work is undertaken**
- **handling Issues**
- **monitoring progress.**

From any of these strands it may be necessary to escalate decision-making to the Project Board, although it is most likely that this will result from Issues. The multiple and overlapping processes within each of these strands can be simplified when viewed from this perspective.

Ensuring that scheduled work is undertaken is closely related to Managing Product Delivery. It can be regarded as the Project Manager's side of Managing Product Delivery. The reader should refer to the Managing Product Delivery section (9.5) within this chapter for more comprehensive discussion of this topic.

Issue handling is often carried out via some form of Issue Log, with formats ranging from simple paper documents in ring-binders to sophisticated databases. More often, Issue handling is carried out verbally. This is not a recommendation but a statement of how projects operate in reality. There is perhaps more verbal reporting when teams are co-located because

Project Managers, by necessity, need to move around between their teams. It is now increasingly commonplace for teams to be geographically dispersed, but the mobile phone has become the medium for Issue handling, retaining verbal reporting. The Project Management team needs to recognise that they are undertaking processes like Capturing Issues (CS3) and Escalating Issues (CS8) when they are participating in such conversations.

How, if at all, should Issues be documented? There is a tendency for unimportant Issues to be documented in Issue Logs, while more important Issues are only handled verbally. Given the profile of significant Issues, this is understandable. Difficulties can then arise subsequently when last week's major Issue reappears and there is no documentation. Consideration should be given to this before the Issues begin to arise because there may not be time to consider the format of Issue Logs once a project is underway.

In a similar vein, escalation via an Exception Report may well be verbal. A confirmatory e-mail may put in place sufficient documentation if it is then filed electronically in the project file. Progress monitoring, involving Checkpoint and Highlight Reports, can be viewed in a similar manner, although it is more likely that a document will be produced.

9.6.4 Implementing

Within Controlling a Stage the format of reports to senior management is most likely to be dependent on the background culture. Organisations have varied styles: young, high-tech companies tend to rely on e-mails; more traditional organisations seem to be more comfortable with formal documentation. There are still areas where people expect reports to be written in what some might now consider an old-fashioned style. Initially, the Project Manager should aim to comply with the underlying culture. However, there can be pitfalls with the overly informal approach, which can lead to insufficient documentation. Equally, there can be problems with a formal approach. There is a tendency to write traditional reports using the passive voice. The danger here is that sentences can be written with no subject. The last sentence illustrates such a vague passive: 'Who writes the sentences?' The Project Manager must ensure that reports are specific about where problems have come from and who is expected to take the next action.

9.7 Managing Stage Boundaries

9.7.1 Cross-reference to the PRINCE2 method

- Managing Stage Boundaries (SB) process and associated management products, notably End Stage Reports

9.7.2 Example

A Project Manager, assisted by the Senior Supplier acting in an assurance role, completed Managing Stage Boundaries in 15 minutes just before a hastily convened Mid-Stage or Exception Assessment. They discussed each process within Managing Stage Boundaries and agreed verbal recommendations. These recommendations were accepted by the subsequent Mid-Stage or Exception Assessment and the Project Manager then incorporated the approved changes into an updated Stage Plan. The pace and informality of this process depended on the close trust among the members of the project management team. It may have been impossible or less likely if circumstances were different.

9.7.3 Scaling

It is of fundamental importance to appreciate the function of management stages when scaling PRINCE2. **Management Stages act as planning boundaries and an opportunity for the Project Board to recommit to the project.**

Where circumstances permit, a project may consist of an initiation stage and only one other stage. The process of Managing Stage Boundaries will then only occur if the project enters Exception. The occasions when multiple stages will not be required are covered in more detail in Section 8.4, *Stages*.

If Managing Stage Boundaries is required, however, it is appropriate to understand the underlying concept beneath the process. Managing Stage Boundaries is an opportunity for both the Project Board and the Project Manager to re-focus on the achievement of business benefit. When doing this, there must also be a review of progress and, therefore, of the quality of products. So, from a very simple test there emerges a much more comprehensive review of the project.

When scaling, it is acceptable in projects where progress and quality are obvious to simplify Managing Stage Boundaries to a review of the Business Case if, that is, it is considered to include risks as well as costs and benefits. Preparation for an End Stage Assessment can therefore be reduced to an Exception Assessment with the Project Board. For any important meeting it is prudent to look at and prepare supporting documentation for each agenda item and to circulate these documents. This is what occurs during Managing Stage Boundaries.

Each of the processes within Managing Stage Boundaries can be equated to the agenda items for an End or Mid-Stage Assessment. This can be a straightforward and brief exercise. More fundamentally, it is a timely reminder to the Project Manager to change focus from the day-to-day control of a stage to a broader view of the project.

Managing Stage Boundaries is also an exercise that has to be carried out between receiving the Project Board's response to an Exception Report and submitting an Exception Plan. During this short period the project will be operating outside the scope of an approved Stage Plan. The Project Board will be aware of this and will be expecting an updated Plan. Consequently, work must be carried out as quickly as possible. It should be possible to create an Exception Plan within days or hours rather than weeks. If such a timescale is acceptable for an Exception Plan then scheduled Stage Plans should take a similar time to produce. The Project Manager must schedule the effort required to undertake Managing Stage Boundaries into the Stage Plan for the preceding Stage.

9.7.4 Implementing

There are likely to be fewer cultural influences on the format of Managing Stage Boundaries. The work is carried out by the Project Manager during time he or she should have scheduled and therefore under his or her control. Cultural influences that are asserted may be indirect, coming from the format of End Stage Assessments and possibly from any external documentation standards that might exist. Some organisations insist that documents are released in advance of meetings. The Project Manager should allow for these lead times when scheduling Managing Stage Boundaries.

9.8 Closing a Project

9.8.1 Cross-reference to the PRINCE2 method

- Closing a Project (CP) process and associated management products, notably Closure Notification, Acceptances, Follow-on Action Recommendations, Post-Project Review Plan, End Project Report and Lessons Learned Report

9.8.2 Example

At the end of a difficult project a quality assurance person was tasked with carrying out a review. This review included elements of Follow-on Action Recommendations, a Lessons Learned Report and an End Project Report. It made a number of political points that were of use in a power struggle that was then taking place between various managers within the organisation. However, it was weak in addressing either Follow-on Actions or Lessons Learned. Consequently, a second project (with a marginal Business Case) was started, which ran for a considerable period.

9.8.3 Scaling

The aims of Closing a Project are to:

- prevent project teams becoming self-sustaining
- ensure no loose ends are left untied
- provide a transition to benefit realisation.

These three aspects are the fundamental principles behind Closing a Project and should be considered when tailoring it. These aims, and the numerous management products produced during Closing a Project, must all be considered against the background of the underlying line culture because after Closing the Project the project environment will no longer exist.

9.8.4 Implementing

Given the number of management products produced from Closing a Project, it may be helpful to consider each and relate them to the aims stated above.

Acceptance documentation ensures that those who will ultimately be responsible for products are content with them. This should always be created in a format that suits the culture of those ultimate custodians of the products. Closure Notification tends to exist where there is a central body that co-ordinates projects. Where such organisations exist, their standards should be complied with.

Follow-on Action Recommendations are the main tool for managing the tendency for project teams to become self-sustaining. Once a project team has formed there is a natural human desire for that team to remain in existence, particularly if it is successful and happy. The continued existence of the team may not be in the wider interests of the business, however. Therefore, some form of 'firebreak' needs to be created to prevent the project team identifying a follow-on project that involves, coincidentally, all the team members. The secondary aim of this document is to identify loose ends, some of which may trigger another project. It is probably best if this identified new project does not involve exactly the same project team.

The End Project Report is a baseline of costs and benefits to date, which provides a starting point for benefit realisation. Projects only exist in order to realise benefits. Therefore, whatever has transpired within the project, the End Project Report and Post-Project Review Plan should be clearly focused on business benefits. The benefit realisation exercise is completed when the Post-Project Review is carried out.

In contrast, the Lessons Learned Report is an inward-looking document reviewing how the project was managed. All too frequently these documents become an opportunity for praise or criticism of Project Managers, depending more on their political influence than on the success of the project. It is extremely useful to have benefits-related documents separated from the Lessons Learned Report as the latter may be politically biased. This is not to say that learning lessons on project management is of no value. Indeed PRINCE2 is no more than the accumulated lessons learned from many projects.

At the end of a project, the project environment wanes and the line environment is reasserted. Cultural influences from the line environment will have a much greater effect on the format of End Project documentation than the scale of a project.

10
SCALING TECHNIQUES

This chapter describes how each individual technique can be reduced in complexity.

10.1 Product-based planning

10.1.1 Cross-reference to the PRINCE2 method

- Product-based planning technique

10.1.2 Overview

All too often Project or Team Managers produce plans in isolation (although the PRINCE2 method recommends that these are communal activities). Isolated planning can lead to the widespread use of scheduling tools and the production of overly complex and detailed documents. There is often an imbalance between light supporting text and the detail found in Gantt charts, with an over-abundance of information at the beginning of a plan and reducing levels towards the end.

These issues are all addressed in the structure of a PRINCE2 plan and in the concept of Levels of Plan. Nevertheless, **new practitioners sometimes interpret the PRINCE2 advice to mean including product-based diagrams as further additions to already complex plans. What they have failed to appreciate is that PRINCE2 advises the reduction of plan complexity in some areas. It is therefore important to understand the specific role of each of the three product-based planning steps.**

Product-based planning is frequently omitted from corporate implementations of PRINCE2. There seem to be three reasons for this. First, it is a skill that must be practised rather than knowledge that can be taught and learnt. Organisations should consider how they can build up this skill in one or more employees. The most successful approach seems to be one that involves the use of external consultants to provide skill transfer to a number of identified staff. Trained staff then become the in-house experts on product-based planning. An approach that encourages all Project Managers to acquire product-based planning skills seems to be less successful.

Secondly, although there are some product-based planning tools on the market they are immature when compared to scheduling tools. Organisations are therefore reluctant to introduce product-based planning support tools.

Thirdly, although staff could pass product-based planning exam questions, they found it did not offer value when used during real projects. The 2002 edition of the PRINCE2 manual includes a significant revision to the advice about product-based planning, which explains how high-level (integration) products can be transferred onto a Product Flow Diagram. This additional information helps projects to identify integration tests. Although this advantage of product-based planning was not specifically excluded from previous editions of the PRINCE2 manual, training organisations were not teaching this approach.

The proper application of product-based planning, as currently understood, can bring additional advantages to projects by anticipating the effort involved in integrating various products towards the ends of projects.

10.1.3 Product Breakdown Structures

10.1.3.1 Example

A hospital trust had to introduce a new IT system before the year 2000. The system linked numerous pieces of analytical equipment on a number of sites.

When a planning workshop was held, a Product Breakdown Structure was created. The team identified that they had to provide training for laboratory staff. This work would take nearly six months, which had to be accommodated within the fixed deadline of the project. Production of a Product Breakdown Structure allowed the team to appreciate the extent of this work at the beginning of the project. The IT department identified the training they required and included it in the Project Plan.

10.1.3.2 Scaling

Product Breakdown Structures assist a project team to:

- identify the scope of a project
- agree the relative importance of different aspects of a project
- coin a common vocabulary.

Where a project has a broad scope, for example one covering the development of business processes and IT systems, these are all necessary activities.

Occasional members of a project team or those given little explanation of Product Breakdown Structures can readily understand such structures and the self-explanatory diagramming conventions used. A Product Breakdown Structure is a very elegant way of demonstrating progress by simply marking completed products on it. Readily available tools, such as presentation packages, can also document Product Breakdown Structures. Although these tools lack integration with scheduling software, their ease of adoption can be an advantage.

10.1.3.3 Implementing

The PRINCE2 champion may find that a Product Breakdown Structure can be useful:

- when there is doubt about the scope of a project
- when the project is truly unique/the first time something is being done
- if there is a history of project failure
- as a communication tool during a planning workshop
- in a subsequent plan, as a record of the consensus reached at the workshop
- as a simple reporting tool, whereby the team mark off completed products.

It is particularly valuable for showing how a number of disparate products come together into higher level, integration products. As a communication tool, it should be created at a workshop involving people from all the disciplines contributing to the project. It should be drafted on a white board or using Post-it Notes™ on a wall. Once typed up, it should then be circulated widely for review to ensure that the full scope of the project has been clarified.

Paradoxically, the simplicity and power of a Product Breakdown Structure can actually hinder its adoption. In some cultures, the clarity of communication is a disadvantage. The Project Manager wishing to introduce Product Breakdown Structures to a Project Board may need to consider how it will be received. There is also a preconception that a Gantt chart must form a major part of a plan, so some Project Boards may feel it is inappropriate to stop producing Gantt charts. They are, however, not mandatory. The champion must take a pragmatic approach; the overriding aim is to establish a rapport between the Project Manager and the Project Board.

Implementation issues can be avoided if the importance of the Product Breakdown Structure is played down. Other members of the team need not be taught the new technique: the Product Breakdown Structure is sufficiently straightforward to be introduced without explanation. **Presentation of a simple yet clear diagram such as a Product Breakdown Structure clarifies communication between the Project Manager and the Project Board on the one hand, and the team on the other.**

10.1.4 Product Descriptions

10.1.4.1 Example

A widely based team was tasked with reviewing their procedures for allocating, monitoring and controlling budgets. The team adopted PRINCE2 with a will and set about generating numerous Product Descriptions. The team embarked on the project and only referred to these Product Descriptions in hindsight. Because they had a PRINCE2 label on them, staff seemed to regard the Product Descriptions as being specialist documents that were not relevant to them.

The project was characterised by numerous meetings but limited progress. When it finished, the project was considered to have been only partially successful. With hindsight, the team members did not understand what the overall outcome was supposed to be. When the Product Descriptions were revisited, all agreed that they had comprehensively documented the project outcomes. Yet, although the team members had participated in writing the Product Descriptions, they did not regard them as being a description of what would be created by the project. Because the Product Descriptions had a PRINCE2 label; team members had not absorbed the implications of their content.

10.1.4.2 Scaling

Product Descriptions are particularly useful for products that:

- have been problematic when produced elsewhere
- will be produced under contract
- are unknown to managers, particularly the Project Manager.

Product Descriptions are also useful on projects that are information-rich. The Purpose, Composition and Derivation headings can assist the user to differentiate packages of information. Composition can, of course, also be shown on a Product Breakdown Structure, and Derivation on a Product Flow Diagram.

Product Descriptions can be regarded as sitting within the product-based planning technique, between Product Breakdown Structures and Product Flow Diagrams. Given this understanding, there is a danger that they are regarded as a specialised planning tool. An alternative view is that they are related to the Quality component. They represent the lowest level at which participants express their Quality Expectations. Some feel Product Descriptions must all be generated at the beginning of a project, during Planning. At this point there may not be clarity of the detailed breakdown of products. Product Descriptions generated early in the project may need to be amended, and the effort in maintaining them means that they fall into disuse.

The PRINCE2 concept of Levels of Plan is often linked to stages and the need for management commitment. But Levels of Plan can also be used to delay the creation of Product Descriptions until more is known about the products to be created. PRINCE2 does allow there to be multiple Levels of Plan below the Stage Plan. When each of these lower-level plans is created, it is an appropriate time to generate lower-level Product Descriptions.

There is also no need to generate Product Descriptions for every single product. Certainly there is limited value in creating Product Descriptions for management products if standard PRINCE2 documents are being used. But, even for specialist products, a balance has to be struck on the level of documentation needed for straightforward products. If the producer and reviewer of a product are clear on what the product will be and how it will be checked, there is limited need for a formal Product Description. Also, if there is a sound technical methodology in place they may be less important.

Considering the above, fewer Product Descriptions need be produced, and they can be produced at different times within the project, for example just before work starts on creating the product itself. In this way staff may feel ownership of the Product Descriptions.

10.1.4.3 Implementing

Specifications are designed to provide detailed information within a specialist group. Product Descriptions are communication tools for use between staff from different specialist groups. A simple analogy will clarify the difference between them. Most readers use cars and will understand the purpose of a car. They could write a Product Description describing how they use the car to travel to and from work, and therefore how they would test a new car. Few of us understand the specification for a car, which would describe, in terms understandable to the automotive engineer, how the car functions.

Within the project there may be products that are similar to those produced for another project. For example, the User Manual for one system could be similar to the User Manual for another; or a piece of hardware provided by a Supplier to one client might be similar to a piece of hardware provided to another. In these circumstances standard specifications may evolve. If the products are to be used within PRINCE2 projects, standard Product Descriptions can also be created and reused with only minor modifications.

10.1.5 Product Flow Diagrams

10.1.5.1 Example

An ambitious project that would affect many users in various different regions was planned without the use of Product Flow Diagrams. There were a large number of constraints on the project but the emphasis during planning was on acquiring sufficient staff. As the project neared the end of system testing it was realised that provision had not been made for an early release of the system to be used for training. The version that was released was unstable. Consequently, the users involved in training became disillusioned with the new system and its implementation was seriously delayed.

10.1.5.2 Scaling

While this book commends the use of Product Breakdown Structures within the majority of projects, particularly those that are broadly based, the situation regarding Product Flow Diagrams is different. It is the identification of dependencies that has most impact on the relevance of an activity network. **Product Flow Diagrams, based on a well-constructed Product Breakdown Structure, are very powerful tools that allow participants in a planning workshop to carry out a sufficiently detailed analysis of dependencies.**

A dependency network is only a model of what will actually happen in a project. This model can be made increasingly accurate during planning if additional effort is expended on analysing all the possible dependencies. In addition, the Project Evaluation and Review Technique (PERT), which is outside the scope of PRINCE2, applies best, worst and median probabilities to dependencies. Within PRINCE2, a less sophisticated approach is adopted whereby a single value is allocated to both activity estimates and to dependencies. Nevertheless, this can be a very rigorous approach to planning if sufficient effort is put into identifying dependencies.

Within the types of project for which PRINCE2 is typically used, for example those with intangible products, dependency analysis tends to be done 'by eye'. Furthermore, critical path analysis, the next step in the planning process, also tends to be done this way, rather than by using the scheduling functions within scheduling tools. Such tools provide little if any support for the identification of dependencies. They do, however, provide considerable assistance in the manipulation of dependencies. Consequently, it is not surprising that instruction manuals and training courses for scheduling tools simply say the user must first identify the dependencies.

The Project Manager, when scaling PRINCE2, must decide the level of accuracy he or she requires for a dependency network. If, in their subjective view and following consultation among the stakeholders, dependencies are straightforward, it is reasonable to question the use of Product Flow Diagrams. If there are likely to be complex dependencies then the use of Product Flow Diagram should be considered. Consideration of the nature of dependencies and analysis of dependency networks should be part of the 'tools of the trade' of Project Managers. The recommendation of this book, therefore, is that Product Flow Diagrams should be used if the Project Manager suspects there are complex dependencies.

10.1.5.3 Implementing

On the one hand, Project Managers may find it difficult to introduce dependency analysis into the hurly-burly of a typical project. Dependency analysis must be done with the active participation of contributors from all the relevant stakeholder groups and this is sometimes difficult to achieve. On the other hand, sites frequently introduce sophisticated scheduling tools and insist that they are used across projects as an input into resource-tracking. Where this is done without adequate dependency and critical path analysis Project Managers become adept at submitting project plans that, though imprecise, give an adequate level of resource availability. Such plans are of limited value when controlling a project.

Dependency and critical path analyses should be carried out during Planning (PL). The *Planning* and *Product-Based Planning* chapters in the manual give useful guidance. It may also be appropriate to enlist the assistance of a product-based planning expert to help the organisation develop these skills. Alternatively, niche training in practical product-based planning is available.

10.2 Change Control Approach

10.2.1 Cross-reference to the PRINCE2 method

- Change Control Approach technique

10.2.2 Example

In the midst of a year 2000 preparation programme a change was logged that more equipment was needed in a company's control room. The cost of the change would be less than £100 within a very large project. Four senior staff spent half an hour debating the change thus spending more in staff time than the cost of the change itself.

10.2.3 Scaling

Once the Change Control policy for a project has been decided there is still a need to implement a Change Control Approach. The PRINCE2 manual describes one such approach in considerable detail. Some argue that there are weaknesses within this approach, which are revealed in a note in the PRINCE2 manual (just before the *Hints and tips* section). The note advises that the term 'Change Authority' should be substituted for 'Project Board' where appropriate within the technique. This note reveals that the Change Control Approach chapter was written before the Change Control component chapter was written or even devised. Therefore, when looked at in detail, the Change Control Approach seems to pre-empt decisions about the delegation of Change Budgets from the Project Board to either a Change Authority or to the Project Manager.

When scaling this technique, there are many variations that can be introduced. Not only can the composition of a Change Authority vary, but the Project Manager may or may not have a delegated Change Budget. In a very small project the Project Board might act as the Change Authority. As projects increase in size, one member of the Project Board, typically the Senior User, could fulfil this function. On larger projects it might be delegated, perhaps to someone from the user community carrying out Project Assurance. In these circumstances that individual would no longer be able to give assurance on Change Control; this function would revert to the Project Board. On even larger projects quite substantial Change Authorities might be formed from staff representing the various stakeholder groups.

In addition, the Project Manager could be delegated the entire Change Budget. This, potentially, presents the Project Manager with difficulties in ensuring that the Project Board does not override decisions on changes. This point should be addressed during Initiation. If there is some split of a Change Budget between a Change Authority and the Project Manager, the rules for allocating changes to the two different budgets need to be carefully defined.

Otherwise, attempts could be made to move changes to one or the other budget, for a variety of reasons. The Change Budget is different from both the contingency budget – which caters for specific risks; and tolerance – which caters for the inevitable differences between the plan and what actually happens. It is unwise to cross-subsidise these budgets. The Project Manager will not be thanked for exceeding tolerance because he or she has been funding unauthorised changes from the core budget.

Only some of these possibilities are covered within the Change Control Approach technique. In Designing a Plan (PL1) the existence of these options is alluded to under the heading of Change Budgets. However the Change Budget is structured, the Project Manager needs to ensure that there are some agreed procedures, whether formal or informal, for escalating changes. Without these, debates about budgets can divert the Project Management team from its primary role.

10.2.4 Implementing

Culturally, those organisations that are people-focused tend to put considerable effort into considering the impact of changes. At the other extreme, organisations with an emphasis on products, for example the engineering profession, will be much more concerned about the budgetary effect of changes. The Project Manager should take into account these cultural influences when agreeing a Change Control Approach.

10.3 Quality Reviews

10.3.1 Cross-reference to the PRINCE2 method

●   Quality Review technique

10.3.2 Example

A project team was operating across a number of sites. The Project Board and Project Assurance were based in the corporate headquarters in London and Project Assurance occasionally visited the various other sites. However, the Project Manager would visit Project Assurance more frequently, while at the company headquarters. He demonstrated progress by discussing documentary output from Quality Reviews with Project Assurance staff.

10.3.3 Scaling

The Quality Review occupies a unique position in the history of PRINCE. It was included in the early days of PRINCE and can be a very powerful tool for ensuring that quality is firmly established. An alternative, periphery view is that it is a bureaucratic and old-fashioned technique. In truth, both of these views are correct. The Quality Review is a very effective tool when used in the right circumstances, however it is simplistic to assert that Quality Reviews should be used every time a product is checked. This is only true if every type of quality check, including informal techniques such as peer review, is recognised as a Quality Review. When asked to proofread a letter most PRINCE2 practitioners would be hard-pressed to equate this with a Quality Review.

There is an implication within the PRINCE2 manual that Quality Reviews should indeed be used every time a product is checked. At various points in the manual it might be more appropriate for the phrase 'quality checked, for example at a Quality Review' to be used in place of the simple term 'Quality Review'. It may be more helpful to regard a Quality Review as a technique to be used only when there are no other recognised and successful quality-checking techniques.

Pragmatically, the champion may care to regard every quality check, however informal, as a scaled Quality Review.

The Quality Review is a very useful procedure for checking products that can be printed on paper, for example documents, reports, specifications or management products. It is useful whenever quality criteria are subjective or involve judgement or, indeed, taste. If criteria are objective or there is a yes/no check, the Quality Review may be rendered unnecessary. The Quality Review is also an effective tool when relations between various stakeholder groups have become strained. A proficient Chairman can reduce the mistrust between groups within a Quality Review. Finally, It is also appropriate to use Quality Reviews when the acceptance of products will lead to major contractual payments. Once the PRINCE2 champion appreciates the circumstances in which Quality Reviews are appropriate, they can be used effectively.

10.3.4 Implementing

Some practitioners assume that Quality Reviews are conducted by the Project Board at an End Stage Assessment. In fact, most Quality Reviews take place within the team during Executing a Work Package (MP2). Quality Reviews must be carried out by reviewers who have the appropriate skills. Control is improved if Reviews (or other checks) are carried out frequently, for example on interim versions of products or on parts of products. As a guide, Quality Reviews should be sufficiently frequent that the Project or Team Manager can judge if they are within Tolerance, based on products being fit for purpose rather just on effort expended. For example, if the Tolerance on a Work Package is one team week, it would be sensible if all the work of the team were reviewed at least every week.

Another aspect of the Quality Review process is that the comprehensive documentation that can be generated from Quality Review can be a useful way of providing an audit trial for inspection by Project Assurance. If Project Assurance come from a Quality Assurance or audit background and are geographically remote, providing them with access to Quality Review documentation can be an elegant way for them to fulfil their role.

When scaling PRINCE2 there can be advantages when involving members of the Project Management team in Quality Reviews if there is a hands-on culture. Project Assurance can carry out Quality Reviews if their Assurance function, for the Review, reverts to the Project Board. If Project Assurance is remote from a project, or if they are criticising the project for political reasons, the Project Manager can often bind them into a project by asking them to undertake Quality Reviews. In a similar manner, the Project Board can undertake reviews of important documents if they have the interest.

10.4 Filing

10.4.1 Cross-reference to the PRINCE2 method

- Filing technique

10.4.2 Example

A company took particular care when implementing PRINCE2 to adopt the same document control procedures and template structures as were used elsewhere within its organisation. Although these were rather more onerous than necessary, when viewed in purely project terms, staff were familiar with these procedures and adopted them without any difficulty. However, when this company began to carry out projects with another company that had less rigorous documentation standards there was some conflict. The second company was unsure whether the additional bureaucracy arose from PRINCE2 or the culture of the first company.

10.4.3 Scaling

As mentioned in Section 7.1.5, *Informality*, filing can be held in any appropriate medium. This can range from a loose-leaf ring-binder on the Project Manager's desk; through traditional paper files; to filing in electronic folders, document management systems, or specialist configuration management tools. **The Project Manager needs to choose an appropriate medium for filing.**

Also, Project Managers or configuration management staff, who may be administrators within Project Support, should consider whether old versions of each product should be kept. If they are to be kept, the length of storage time and whether they should be archived need to be considered.

10.4.4 Implementing

Filing is an aspect of implementing Configuration Management. Some sectors are very familiar with configuration management and are likely to have adequate configuration management procedures in place. The PRINCE2 champion need only adopt these procedures for the project. Other industry sectors may be unfamiliar with configuration management and may even find the concept of filing alien. The Project Manager needs to adapt the project filing strategy both to the needs of project and to the impending impact on company culture.

11
A MINIMALIST PRINCE2 PROJECT

Some readers may find it difficult to imagine scaling PRINCE2 in the manner described in the preceding chapters. To help to convince them, a fictitious example of a project is detailed below, showing PRINCE2 scaled down to the absolute minimum but still fully and recognisably PRINCE2. A 20-person-day project is described, which is controlled informally but uses a complete range of PRINCE2 elements. Cross-references to specific PRINCE2 elements are given in parentheses. Abbreviations are used freely so the reader may want to study this chapter alongside the PRINCE2 manual and, in particular, the context diagrams for the eight high-level processes.

The example is deliberately condensed to what might be considered the bare bones of PRINCE2. In this way, the most lightweight possible implementation of the method can be illustrated, though as such it will be rather atypical. None the less it demonstrates how the principles of PRINCE2 remain true, relevant and operable, however large or small the context.

11.1 Example

Jack and Jill are two directors of a small company with half a dozen staff. They work together in a single open-plan office. They think of a piece of work for use by the company in the future. As yet, there are no specific customers for this product. The details of this specialist product need not concern us but the format of the product will be some sort of electronic file.

11.1.1 Controlled Start

In response to the idea that has emerged (Project Mandate), Jack and Jill decide to discuss the project. They first decide what they want from the project (Quality Expectations in Project Brief). They agree that they could do all the work themselves (SU5 and Project Approach). Jack has greater availability in the next month so he will act as Project Manager and the specialist team. No Team Manager or Project Support will be needed. Jill will act as Project Board and Project Assurance (SU1, SU2, SU3 and Organisation). Within the same meeting (therefore no SU4, Project Brief, SU6 or DP1), they agree that Jill will check Jack's work (IP1; Quality Plan; Quality, Configuration Management and Change Control).

On a piece of paper (PL1) they jot down a few thoughts about the final product and its contents (a Product Description and Product Breakdown Structure). They can see immediately (no Product Flow Diagram) the composition and sequence of the final product (PL2, PL3 and Stage Selection). They add some estimates to a hand-written plan (Project and Stage Plan, PL4, PL5). They do not feel much is likely to go wrong (PL6) and move on (PL7). Jack writes a few hand-written notes (IP6).

They agree it is worth spending 10 person days on this project (IP3 and Business Case), but it could overrun by up to one day (Tolerance). They decide that they can chat frequently (IP4 and Controls). Jack states which electronic folder he will use for storing documents and where he will keep the ring-binder with any paper documents, including the notes of this meeting (DP2).

11.1.2 Controlled Progress

Jack thinks about what he needs to do (CS1 and MP1) and sets to work, showing Jill various drafts (MP2). When he has made the necessary corrections he puts completed documents in a sub-folder (MP3 and CS9). Every few days he looks back at the Plan (CS2). No Issues have emerged (CS3, CS4 and CS8) so he considers his next task (CS7) and mentions that all is well to Jill (CS6 and DP4).

11.1.3 Controlled Close

The work proceeds smoothly in this vein (no SB or DP3). When the work is finished, Jack moves the final document into another folder where his colleagues can have access to it (CP1). He agrees with Jill that they should check in six months whether the product has been useful (CP2). They agree that they were within budget and PRINCE2 was an effective project management tool (CP3 and DP5).

11.2 Conclusion

This example illustrates the use of an Initiation Stage and only one other Stage. Consequently, Stage Boundaries will be omitted, if the project proceeds according to plan. Maximum use is made of informal and verbal plans and controls. Within such a small project configuration management, issue management and risk management are straightforward. While this may seem a deliberately extreme example, it is similar to any number of small PRINCE2 projects. Nevertheless, this example is intended to be a good example of tailoring PRINCE2. The method has been implemented in a way that suits this culture, and has been scaled in the light of one particular project. The result is a light yet comprehensive project management environment that assisted those involved to manage a successful project.

GLOSSARY

Acceptance Criteria

A prioritised list of criteria that the final product(s) must meet before the customer will accept them; a measurable definition of what must be done for the final product to be acceptable to the customer. They should be defined as part of the Project Brief and agreed between customer and supplier no later than the project initiation stage. They should be documented in the Project Initiation Document.

Activity network

A flow diagram showing the activities of a plan and their interdependencies. The network shows each activity's duration, earliest start and finish times, latest start and finish times and float. Also known as 'planning network'. *See also* Critical path.

Baseline

A snapshot; a position or situation that is recorded. Although the position may be updated later, the baseline remains unchanged and available as a reminder of the original state and as a comparison against the current position. Products that have passed their quality checks and are approved are baselined products. Anything 'baselined' should be under version control in configuration management and 'frozen', i.e. no changes to that version are allowed.

Benefits

The positive outcomes, quantified or unquantified, that a project is being undertaken to deliver, and that justify the investment.

Benefits realisation

The practice of ensuring that the outcome of a project produces the projected benefits claimed in the Business Case.

Business Case

Information that describes the justification for setting up and continuing a PRINCE2 project. It provides the reasons (and answers the question 'Why?') for the project. It is updated at key points throughout the project.

Change authority

A group to which the Project Board may delegate responsibility for the consideration of requests for change. The change authority is given a budget and can approve changes within that budget.

124

Change budget

The money allocated to the change authority to be spent on authorised requests for change.

Change control

The procedure to ensure that the processing of all Project Issues is controlled, including the submission, analysis and decision-making.

Checkpoint

A team-level, time-driven review of progress, usually involving a meeting.

Checkpoint Report

A progress report of the information gathered at a checkpoint meeting, which is given by a team to the Project Manager and provides reporting data as defined in the Work Package.

Communication Plan

Part of the Project Initiation Document describing how the project's stakeholders and interested parties will be kept informed during the project.

Concession

An Off-Specification that is accepted by the Project Board without corrective action.

Configuration audit

A comparison of the latest version number and status of all products shown in the configuration library records against the information held by the product authors.

Configuration management

A discipline, normally supported by software tools, that gives management precise control over its assets (for example, the products of a project), covering planning, identification, control, status accounting and verification of the products.

Configuration status account

A report on the status of products. The required products can be specified by identifier or the part of the project in which they were developed.

Contingency budget

The amount of money required to implement a contingency plan. If the Project Board approves a contingency plan, it would normally set aside a contingency budget, which would only be called upon if the contingency plan had to be implemented.

Contingency plan

A plan that provides an outline of decisions and measures to be taken if defined circumstances, outside the control of a PRINCE2 project, should occur.

Critical path

This is the line connecting the start of a planning network with the final activity in that network through those activities with the smallest float. Often this is a line through the network connecting those activities with a zero float, i.e. those activities where any delay will delay the time of the entire network.

Customer

The person or group who commissioned the work and will benefit from the end results.

Deliverable

An item that the project has to create as part of the requirements. It may be part of the final outcome or an intermediate element on which one or more subsequent deliverables are dependent. According to the type of project, another name for a deliverable is 'product'.

End Project Report

A report given by the Project Manager to the Project Board, that confirms the hand-over of all products and provides an updated Business Case and an assessment of how well the project has done against its Project Initiation Document.

End stage assessment

The review by the Project Board and Project Manager of the End Stage Report to decide whether to approve the next Stage Plan (unless the last stage has now been completed). According to the size and criticality of the project, the review may be formal or informal. The approval to proceed should be documented as an important management product.

End Stage Report

A report given by the Project Manager to the Project Board at the end of each management stage of the project. This provides information about the project performance during the stage and the project status at stage end.

Exception

A situation where it can be forecast that there will be a deviation beyond the tolerance levels agreed between Project Manager and Project Board (or between Project Board and corporate or programme management, or between a Team Manager and the Project Manager).

Exception assessment

This is a meeting of the Project Board to approve (or reject) an Exception Plan.

Exception Plan

This is a plan that often follows an Exception Report. For a Stage Plan exception, it covers the period from the present to the end of the current stage. If the exception were at a project level, the Project Plan would be replaced.

Exception Report

A report that describes an exception, provides an analysis and options for the way forward and identifies a recommended option. The Project Manager presents it to the Project Board.

Executive

The single individual with overall responsibility for ensuring that a project or programme meets its objectives and delivers the projected benefits. This individual should ensure that the project or programme maintains its business focus, that it has clear authority and that the work, including risks, is actively managed. The chairperson of the Project Board, representing the customer and owner of the Business Case.

Feasibility study

A feasibility study is an early study of a problem to assess if a solution is feasible. The study will normally scope the problem, identify and explore a number of solutions and make a recommendation on what action to take. Part of the work in developing options is to calculate an outline Business Case for each as one aspect of comparison.

Follow-on Action Recommendations

A report that can be used as input to the process of creating a Business Case/Project Mandate for any follow-on PRINCE2 project and for recording any follow-on instructions covering incomplete products or outstanding issues. It also sets out proposals for post-project review of the project's products.

Gantt chart

This is a diagram of a plan's activities against a time background, showing start and end times and resources required.

Gate review

A generic term, rather than a PRINCE2 term, meaning a point at the end of a stage or phase where a decision is made whether to continue with the project. In PRINCE2 this would equate to an end stage assessment.

Highlight Report

Report from the Project Manager to the Project Board on a time-driven frequency on stage progress.

Issue Log

A log of all Project Issues including requests for change raised during the project, showing details of each issue, its evaluation, what decisions about it have been made and its current status.

Lessons Learned Report

A report that describes the lessons learned in undertaking the project and that includes statistics from the quality control of the project's management products. It is approved by the Project Board and then held centrally for the benefit of future projects.

Off-Specification

Something that should be provided by the project, but currently is not (or is forecast not to be) provided. This might be a missing product or a product not meeting its specification.

Outcome

The term used to describe the totality of what the project is set up to deliver, consisting of all the specialist products. For example, this could be an installed computer system with trained staff to use it, backed up by new working practices and documentation, a refurbished and equipped building with all the staff moved in and working, or it could be a new product launched with a recruited and trained sales and support team in place.

Peer review

Peer reviews are specific reviews of a project or any of its products where personnel from within the organisation and/or from other organisations carry out an independent assessment of the project. Peer reviews can be done at any point within a project but are often used at stage-end points.

Phase

A part, section or segment of a project, similar in meaning to a PRINCE2 stage. The key meaning of stage in PRINCE2 terms is the use of management stages, i.e. sections of the project to which the Project Board only commits one at a time. A phase might be more connected to a time slice, change of skills required or change of emphasis.

Post-implementation review

See Post-project review.

Post-project review

One or more reviews held after project closure to determine if the expected benefits have been obtained. Also known as 'post-implementation review'.

PRINCE2

A method that supports some selected aspects of project management. The acronym stands for **PR**ojects **IN** **C**ontrolled **E**nvironments.

PRINCE2 project

A project whose product(s) can be defined at its start sufficiently precisely so as to be measurable against predefined metrics and that is managed according to the PRINCE2 method.

Process

That which must be done to bring about a particular outcome, in terms of information to be gathered, decisions to be made and results that must be achieved.

Producer

This role represents the creator(s) of a product that is the subject of a quality review. Typically, it will be filled by the person who has produced the product or who has led the team responsible.

Product

Any input to or output from a project. PRINCE2 distinguishes between management products (which are produced as part of the management or quality processes of the project) and specialist products (which are those products that make up the final deliverable). A product may itself be a collection of other products.

Product-based planning

A three-step diagrammatic technique leading to a comprehensive plan based on creation and delivery of required outputs. The technique considers prerequisite products, quality requirements and the dependencies between products.

Product Breakdown Structure

A hierarchy of all the products to be produced during a plan.

Product Checklist

A list of the major products of a plan, plus key dates in their delivery.

Product Description

A description of a product's purpose, composition, derivation and quality criteria. It is produced at planning time, as soon as the need for the product is identified.

Product Flow Diagram

A diagram showing the sequence of production and interdependencies of the products listed in a Product Breakdown Structure.

Programme

A portfolio of projects selected, planned and managed in a co-ordinated way.

Project

A temporary organisation that is created for the purpose of delivering one or more business products according to a specified Business Case.

Project Assurance

The Project Board's responsibilities to assure itself that the project is being conducted correctly.

Project Brief

A description of what the project is to do; a refined and extended version of the Project Mandate, which has been agreed by the Project Board and which is input to project initiation.

Project closure notification

Advice from the Project Board to inform the host location that the project resources can be disbanded and support services, such as space, equipment and access, demobilised.

Project closure recommendation

Notification prepared by the Project Manager for the Project Board to send (when the Board is satisfied that the project can be closed) to any organisation that has supplied facilities to the project.

Project Initiation Document (PID)

A logical document which brings together the key information needed to start the project on a sound basis and to convey that information to all concerned with the project.

Project Issue

A term used to cover either a general issue, query, a Request for Change, suggestion or Off-Specification raised during a project. Project Issues can be about anything to do with the project.

Project management

The planning, monitoring and control of all aspects of the project and the motivation of all those involved in it to achieve the project objectives on time and to the specified cost, quality and performance.

Project management team

A term to represent the entire management structure of Project Board, Project Manager, plus any Team Manager, Project Assurance and Project Support roles.

Project Manager

The person given the authority and responsibility to manage the project on a day-to-day basis to deliver the required products within the constraints agreed with the Project Board.

Project Mandate

Information created externally to the project, which forms the terms of reference and is used to start up the PRINCE2 project.

Project Plan

A high-level plan showing the major products of the project, when they will be delivered and at what cost. An initial Project Plan is presented as part of the Project Initiation Document. This is revised as information on actual progress appears. It is a major control document for the Project Board to measure actual progress against expectations.

Project Quality Plan

A plan defining the key quality criteria, quality control and audit processes to be applied to project management and specialist work in the PRINCE2 project. It will be part of the text in the Project Initiation Document.

Project records

A collection of all approved management, specialist and quality products and other material, which is necessary to provide an auditable record of the project.

NB. This does not include working files.

Project start-up notification

Advice to the host location that the project is about to start and requesting any required Project Support services.

Project Support Office

A group set up to provide certain administrative services to the Project Manager. Often the group provides its services to many projects in parallel.

Quality

The totality of features and characteristics of a product or service that bear on its ability to satisfy stated and implied needs. Also defined as 'fitness for purpose' or 'conforms to requirements'.

Quality Management System

The complete set of quality standards, procedures and responsibilities for a site or organisation.

Quality review

A quality review is a quality checking technique with a specific structure, defined roles and procedure designed to ensure a product's completeness and adherence to standards. The participants are drawn from those with an interest in the product and those with the necessary skills to review its correctness. An example of the checks made by a quality review is 'Does the document match the quality criteria in the Product Description?'

Quality system

See Quality Management System.

Request for Change

A means of proposing a modification to the current specification of a product. It is one type of Project Issue.

Reviewer

A person asked to review a product that is the subject of a quality review.

Risk Log

A document that provides identification, estimation, impact evaluation and countermeasures for all risks to the project. It should be created during the start-up of the project and developed during the life of the project. Also known as 'Risk Register'.

Risk profile

A graphical representation of information normally found on the Risk Log.

Risk register

See Risk Log.

Senior Responsible Owner
This is not a PRINCE2 term, but is used in many organisations. Its equivalent in PRINCE2 terms would be the 'Executive' role.

Senior Supplier
The Project Board role that provides knowledge and experience of the main discipline(s) involved in the production of the project's deliverable(s). Represents the supplier(s) interests within the project and provides supplier resources.

Senior User
A member of the Project Board, accountable for ensuring that user needs are specified correctly and that the solution meets those needs.

Sponsor
Not a specific PRINCE2 role but often used to mean the major driving force of a project. May be the equivalent of 'Executive' or corporate/programme management.

Stakeholders
Parties with an interest in the execution and outcome of a project. They would include business streams affected by or dependent on the outcome of a project.

Supplier
The group or groups responsible for the supply of the project's specialist products.

Team Manager
A role that may be employed by the Project Manager or a specifically appointed alternative person to manage the work of project team members.

Tolerance
The permissible deviation above and below a plan's estimate of time and cost without escalating the deviation to the next level of management. Separate tolerance figures should be given for time and cost. There may also be tolerance levels for quality, scope, benefit and risk. Tolerance is applied at project, stage and team levels.

User(s)
The person or group who will use the final deliverable(s) of the project.

Work Package
The set of information relevant to the creation of one or more products. It will contain the Product Description(s), details of any constraints on production such as time and cost, interfaces and confirmation of the agreement between the Project Manager and the person or Team Manager who is to implement the Work Package that the work can be done within the constraints.

INDEX

Note: The index does not contain references to the Glossary.